# The Nibelungenlied

## Twayne's World Authors Series
### German Literature

Ulrich Weisstein, Editor
*Indiana University*

TWAS 712

Niemam hagen allaine vnd gunther der kunig her
ff Owe lieber wolffhart fol ich dich han verlorn
fo mag mich Immer rewen das ich ye ward geborn
Dyfftab vnd wulfwein vnd auch wolffrant
wer fol mir danne helffen in der ammelunge lant
ff wolffreich der vil chune vnd ift mir der erfchlagen
gehart vnd wikhart wie fol ich die verclagen
Daz ift an meinen frewden zur der lefte tag
Owe daz vor laide niemat zefterben mag

*Dietrich von Bern overpowers Hagen while Kriemhild looks on.*
*Background: Two knights (perhaps Hildebrand and Gunther) in combat.*
*Source: Hundeshagen Codex, MS Germ. Fol. 855,*
    *Staatsbibliothek Preussischer Kulturbesitz*

# The Nibelungenlied

## By Winder McConnell

*University of California at Davis*

*Twayne Publishers* • *Boston*

*The Nibelungenlied*

Winder McConnell

Copyright © 1984 by G. K. Hall & Company
All Rights Reserved
Published by Twayne Publishers
A Division of G. K. Hall & Company
70 Lincoln Street
Boston, Massachusetts 02111

Book Production by Marne B. Sultz

Book Design by Barbara Anderson

Printed on permanent/durable acid-free
paper and bound in the United States of
America.

**Library of Congress Cataloging in Publication Data.**

McConnell, Winder.
    The Nibelungenlied.

    (Twayne's world authors series ; TWAS 712. German
literature)
    Bibliography: p. 132
    Includes index.
    1. Nibelungenlied. I. Title.
II. Series: Twayne's world authors series ; TWAS 712.
III. Series: Twayne's world authors series.
German literature.
PT1589.M37 1984        831'.2        83–27111
ISBN 0–8057–6559–X

For
*Ernst S. Dick*

# Contents

# About the Author

Winder McConnell was born in Belfast, Ireland, in 1945. His undergraduate work was done at McGill University, Montreal, and he holds an M.A. and a Ph.D. from the University of Kansas at Lawrence, where he studied with Ernst S. Dick. He has held teaching and research positions with the University of Western Ontario, Stanford University, the Johns Hopkins University, and is currently associate professor of German at the University of California at Davis.

His publications include a monograph on *The Wate Figure in Medieval Tradition* (Stanford German Studies, 1978), and articles on the heroic epic and *Spielmannsepik*.

# Acknowledgments

Several colleagues provided me with the benefit of their erudition and good judgment during various stages of the book's production: Ernst Dick (Kansas), Stephen Jaeger (Bryn Mawr), Harold Jantz (Duke), Rolf Mueller (Missouri, St. Louis), Alain Renoir (Berkeley), Peter Schaeffer (Davis), Frank Tobin (Nevada, Reno), and David Wells (Queen's University, Belfast). Ulrich Weisstein proved to be an exemplary editor, who combined critical acumen with experienced guidance. My research assistants, Ursula D'Angelo and Michele Van Vranken, logged many hours in libraries and in the organization of the bibliography. Completion of the manuscript was facilitated by several research grants and a sabbatical leave from the University of California at Davis, as well as through the untiring services of Inge Heuser and Helene Schaffron of the Department of German. To all of the above, as well as to numerous others with whom I have discussed the subject over the past three years, I express my sincere thanks. I am grateful, as well, to my wife, Kathy, and my daughter, Karen, for their patience and understanding, and for helping to insure that this labor of love was not "mit leide . . . verendet."

# Abbreviations

# Introduction

Gottfried Weber has suggested that a "true" history of *Nibelungenlied* scholarship could easily fill several volumes.[1] A glance at the entries on the epic in the *MLA Bibliography* and *Germanistik* over the past decade or two should suffice to demonstrate that the *Nibelungenlied* still has a formidable appeal for scholars of the Middle Ages. Among the hundreds of articles and dozens of books written on the subject, several authors and specific directions taken by research stand out and deserve more than a fleeting allusion. The debt owed by contemporary scholars to previous researchers is considerable, and knowledge of their achievements, particularly in the area of manuscript retrieval and the production of critical texts, can hardly fail to evoke a profound sense of gratitude and humility. Many of the theories concerning the "original" manuscript or the ultimate origins of the epic have been refuted; others continue to generate controversy, and new issues have emerged to challenge the interpretive skills of scholars. It seems warranted, then, by way of an introduction, to offer a brief, descriptive account of the major trends of *Nibelungenlied* scholarship over the past two centuries.

The first reference to the *Nibelungenlied* to be found in modern German literature is in Hans Jacob Wagner von Wagenfels's *Ehren-Ruff Teütsch-Lands* (Germany's Honor Roll, 1692), in which one reads of "Seyuridt der viel Chune" ("valiant Siegfried") who, in magnificent attire, journeys "in Gunthers Lant" ("to the land of Gunther").[2] In 1755, encouraged by the Swiss, Johann Jacob Bodmer, Jacob Hermann Obereit, a medical doctor in Lindau, paid a visit to the library of the count of Hohenems in Vorarlberg. His finds there included a *Nibelungenlied* manuscript. One year later, Bodmer reported the discovery in the Zürich publication, *Freymüthige Nachrichten von neuen Büchern und anderen zur Gelehrtheit gehörigen Sachen* (Candid reviews of new books and other scholarly publications). In 1757, a partial printing of the manuscript appeared under the title, *Chriemhilden Rache, und die Klage: zwey Heldengedichte aus dem schwäbischen Zeitpunkte. Samt Fragmenten aus dem Gedichte von den Nibelungen und aus dem Josaphat* (Kriemhild's Revenge and The Lament: Two heroic poems from the Swabian era. With fragments

from the Nibelung poem and from Josaphat).[3] The first complete
printing of the *Nibelungenlied* did not occur until a quarter of a
century later. The editor, Christoph Heinrich Müller, a friend of
Bodmer, dedicated the publication to Frederick the Great, who was
not impressed. In a letter dated 22 February 1784, he intimated to
Müller that his literary anthology, which included works from the
twelfth, thirteenth, and fourteenth centuries, was not worth "a shot
of powder." Frederick's sentiments found no echo among serious
scholars. To be sure, Müller's edition had appeared at a time when
reverence for Greek literature had peaked in Germany, but with the
emergence of a national self-respect, furthered in the literary sphere
by Klopstock and Herder, the *Nibelungenlied* quickly gained prominence as testimony to a literary heritage of which the Germans
could justly be proud. Another Swiss, Johannes von Müller, referred
to the epic as the "German Iliad."

Scholarly attention accorded the German Middle Ages was significantly boosted through the publication, in 1799, of Novalis's
*Die Christenheit oder Europa* (Christianity or Europe). Four years later,
Ludwig Tieck published his *Minnelieder aus dem schwäbischen Zeitalter*
(Love poems from the Swabian era), a work which was to have
decisive influence on the later career of Jacob Grimm. The efforts
of the romanticists to extol the quality of earlier German literature
were enhanced by the wave of patriotism in Germany subsequent
to the Peace of Luneville (9 February 1801), as a result of which
the left bank of the Rhine was ceded to France. The fact that German
nobles were to be compensated for the loss of their holdings did
little to temper anti-French sentiment. In the same year, August
Wilhelm Schlegel began to deliver his famous lectures on belles
lettres and art in Berlin. He regarded the *Nibelungenlied* as the
expression of the collective genius of an entire epoch, a work too
great to be the product of a single author. A remarkable fusion of
history and poetry, the *Nibelungenlied* reflected, in Schlegel's opinion, the German national character. In a different sense, this sentiment was echoed over one hundred fifty years later in the biting
sarcasm of Joachim Fernau's *Disteln für Hagen: Bestandsaufnahme der
deutschen Seele* (Thistles for Hagen: A stock-taking of the German
soul).[4]

Whatever the shortcomings of early commentaries and editions,
by the end of the eighteenth century the *Nibelungenlied* had been
lifted, quite literally, from the dust of oblivion and had begun to

command the attention of the leading minds of the period. Goethe, who had known of its existence since his visit to Bodmer in November 1779, and who had received a copy of Christoph Heinrich Müller's edition, began an extensive study of the epic after Friedrich Heinrich von der Hagen sent him a copy of his edition of *Der Nibelungen Lied* in 1807. For the following two years, Goethe occupied himself with the work. In his posthumously published commentary to the Karl Simrock translation of 1827, he maintained that knowledge of the poem constituted an integral part of the nation's education.[5] Von der Hagen's edition was greeted with enthusiasm by the Grimm brothers, and it was reviewed by Jacob Grimm in the *Neuer literarischer Anzeiger* of 1807 and by Wilhelm Grimm in the *Heidelberger Jahrbücher* of 1809.

There were, of course, skeptics, foremost among them August Wilhelm Kotzebue, who maintained that the *Nibelungenlied* was simply a foolish fairy tale, lacking spirit, feeling, and imagination. But at the highpoint of romanticism, critics such as Kotzebue found themselves in a decided minority. The "spirit" of the *Nibelungenlied* was proclaimed in public lectures delivered by von der Hagen in Breslau in 1812, as well as in university lectures by August Zeune in Berlin. By 1816, lectures on the *Nibelungenlied* were offered at the universities of Breslau, Göttingen, Greifswald, and Giessen, while in Heidelberg, Worms, and Frankfurt, large crowds were attracted to the public lectures held by Zeune. Nationalist idealism found expression in the desire of young Germans to march into war against Napoleon with copies of Zeune's *Felt- und Zeltausgabe* (Field edition) of the *Nibelungenlied* in their packs.

*Nibelungenlied* research in the nineteenth century may be said to revolve, in large part, around the achievements of one man, Karl Lachmann, and the subsequent controversy about the theories he proposed concerning the "origins" of the epic. Lachmann (1793–1851) had been trained as a classical philologist and was greatly influenced by the hypothesis advanced by Friedrich August Wolff in his *Prolegomena ad Homerum* (1795), in which the author maintained that the *Iliad* and the *Odyssey* were not the work of one man, but rather compilations of individual rhapsodies through which shorter sections of the epics had previously been orally transmitted. In his *Habilitationsschrift* of 1816, entitled *Über die ursprüngliche Gestalt des Gedichtes von der Nibelungen Noth* (The original form of the poem, "The tragedy of the Nibelungs"), Lachmann suggested that the *Nibelungenlied* had originated through the compilation of individual *Lieder,* formerly independent of one another, and all composed by different poets. Twenty years later, he maintained in his *Anmerkungen zu den Nibelungen und zur Klage* (Notes on the Nibelungen and The Lament) that the original number of *Lieder* had been twenty. Of the three major manuscripts, he considered A (the Hohenems-München manuscript), to be the closest to the original version of the epic because of its many errors and general lack of "polish." In asserting that the *Nibelungenlied* was not the work of an individual author, Lachmann was expressing the same sentiment held by many romanticists, most notably A. W. Schlegel, Tieck, and the Grimm brothers.

Lachmann's theory was not universally accepted. Friedrich Heinrich von der Hagen and Wilhelm Müller took issue with him,[6] the former claiming that the poem was a unified work of art, the latter attempting something of a compromise by suggesting that eight (rather than twenty) *Lieder* had constituted the basis of the epic. In 1854, Adolf Holtzmann in Heidelberg and Friedrich Zarncke in Leipzig expressed a preference for manuscript C (the Donaueschingen manuscript) over manuscript A, and also disputed the multiple authorship proposed by Lachmann.[7] Both were severely criticized by Karl Müllenhoff who, in his eagerness to "defend" Lachmann and his *Liedertheorie,* allowed personal invective to interfere with objective counterargumentation. Nonetheless, resistance to the Lachmann hypothesis increased during the second half of the nineteenth century and on into the twentieth. Among those who helped to lay the theory to rest were Karl Bartsch, who maintained that manuscript B (the St. Gallen manuscript) and C (the Donaueschingen manuscript) could be traced independently to a lost original,[8] Wilhelm Braune, whose careful investigation of all the manuscripts led him to conclude that B was the original version,[9] and, finally, Andreas Heusler, whose name will "forever signify a milestone in *Nibelungenlied* research."[10]

Heusler (1865–1940) had been influenced by W. P. Ker, particularly the latter's *Epic and Romance,* and called for a clear distinction to be made between a "Lied" and an "epic," specifically with regard to the form of narration. The *Lied* commanded a condensed, suggestive, and fleeting style, whereas the epic tended to present the narrative at a leisurely pace, giving considerably more attention to detail. Heusler did not dispute that there was a development from *Lied* to epic, but he asserted that the latter was not simply the compilation of a series of individual *Lieder,* but rather the extension of a single *Lied.* In his *Lied und Epos in germanischer Sagendichtung* ("Lied" and epic in the Germanic sagas),[11] he compared the relationship of the epic to *Lied* to that between the adult and the embryo. Heusler thus disagreed with Lachmann's assumption that *Lieder* were episodic in nature, and claimed that they did, in fact, contain an entire fable. In his later work, *Nibelungensage und Nibelungenlied: Die Stoffgeschichte des deutschen Heldenepos* (Nibelungen saga and Nibelungenlied: The subject matter of the German heroic epic),[12] he suggested that five poets had created the *Nibelungenlied,* two of them composing different versions of a *Brünhildsage* (dating from the fifth/sixth and twelfth centuries respectively), while three others had worked on the *Burgundensage* (fifth, eighth, and twelfth centuries). In Heusler's view, a sixth poet, a *Spielmann,* had combined the two traditions sometime during the first five years of the thirteenth century.

Heusler's theory enjoyed widespread popularity and left little room for further advocacy of Lachmann's *Lieder* hypothesis. Heusler, however, never regarded his thesis to be the "final word" on the subject. Nevertheless, his views dominated *Nibelungenlied* research for decades. Contemporary scholars recognize the importance of Heusler's contribution to this particularly complex area of literary investigation, but are reluctant to accept the basic premise without reservation.[13] Franz Rolf Schröder has maintained that Heusler drew too sharp a distinction between *Lied* and epic, and that he did not pay sufficient attention to "transitional forms." There are indeed *Lieder* (designated *Aventiuren* in the text) which one may well describe as "episodic" in nature, while others contain a longer series of events and are more accurately described as "epics."[14]

Perhaps the most significant contribution to appear on this subject in Germany during World War II was Dietrich von Kralik's *Die Sigfridtrilogie im Nibelungenlied und in der Thidrekssaga* (The Siegfried trilogy in the Nibelungenlied and in the Thidreks saga).[15] Von Kralik's study represents an attempt to move beyond Heusler while at the same time acknowledging the profound debt owed the latter. Von Kralik believed that the *Nibelungenlied* could be directly associated with a far greater number of older heroic lays than Heusler had imagined. His work is, in essence, more an "extension" of Heusler's theory than a contradiction thereof. The *Nibelungenlied* represented the amalgamation of several lays which had existed simultaneously: the "Lay of Grimhild," the "Lay of Brünhild," and the "Lay of Siegfried's Wedding," comprising the first part of the epic, while the second was based on the "Revenge of Grimhild" and the "Demise of the Nibelungs."

The first major commentary on the *Nibelungenlied, Die Klage* (The lament), contains a reference (in the version appended to manuscript B) to the commissioning of a Latin version of the epic by Bishop Pilgrim of Passau. The recipient of the commission was a clerk in the service of Pilgrim, "meister Kuonrat" ("Master Conrad"). Friedrich Zarncke assumed the existence of an earlier Latin version of the epic, while Karl Müllenhoff disputed the information provided by the anonymous author of *Die Klage*. In 1909, Gustav Roethe published an essay entitled "Nibelungias und Waltharius"[16] in which he maintained that the ninth-century *Waltharius* might have inspired the awarding of a commission to Master Conrad to prepare a Latin rendition of the *Nibelung Saga* (the *Nibelungias*), and that this work, when translated into German, served as the basis for the *Nibelungenlied* as it has been passed down to us. Roethe regarded the final scribe as an uneducated *Spielmann,* devoid of any real talent. The argument as to whether or not there may, in fact, have been a Latin precursor to the *Nibelungenlied* is no longer a matter of great concern to scholars, although, at the time, Roethe was not alone in his views.

Apart from the diversity of opinions concerning the original format or "line of development" of the *Nibelungenlied,* there arose the intriguing question as to the ultimate "roots" of the work and its principal characters. Three major theories have been advanced throughout the nineteenth and twentieth centuries: (1) the *Nibelungenlied* is based on actual historical events; (2) the origins of the work are to be sought in the realm of the fairy tale; (3) the *Nibelungenlied* is the heroization of a myth. The historical interpretation of the epic is the oldest, having been advanced by the lawyer and historian Marquard Freher in his *Origines Palatinae* (The origins of the Palatinate) in 1599, in which he stated that the saga of Siegfried was nothing less than distorted history. Siegfried of Xanten was associated with King Sigibert, a Merovingian king of the sixth century, who was murdered in 575. Among those who regarded Siegfried as the fictional embodiment of the historical Sigibert were Karl Wilhelm Göttling,[17] Julius Leichtlen (who suggested that

Siegfried was actually a combination of four or five historical Sigiberts),[18] Emil Rückert (who regarded Siegfried as the fusion of two Sigiberts),[19] Ludwig Ernst,[20] and the noted historian and literary scholar, Georg Gottfried Gervinus.[21] Gregor Sarrazin considered the description of the war against the Saxons and Danes in the fourth *Aventiure* of the *Nibelungenlied* a poetic recounting of the victory won by the Franks over the Saxons and the Danes centuries earlier.[22] A peculiar twist to the historical interpretation of the work was offered by A. Crüger, who attempted to associate major characters with figures prominent in Roman history around the beginning of the fourth century.[23] Siegfried was also identified with St. Victor of Xanten.[24] Many believed the literary hero to be the poetic realization of the historical Hermann, leader of the Cheruscans, who decimated Roman legions under Varus in the Battle of Teutoburg Forest in the year 9 A.D. (Franz Joseph Mone, Adolf Giesebrecht, Rudolf Much, and Hermann Jellinghaus). Siegfried's fight with the dragon was considered to be the abstract depiction of the battle between German and Roman forces, and the winding, Roman columns were felt by some to have provided the concrete base for the image of the slithering dragon. The second half of the epic, which depicts the demise of the Burgundians and Huns, is accepted today by most scholars as the poetic rendering of the actual slaughter of Burgundians under King Gundahari in the year 437 by a Hunnish army, albeit not under the command of Attila.

In the twentieth century, Heusler's name lent considerable authority to the historical interpretation of the *Nibelungenlied*. Hermann Schneider also supported a historical interpretation, as did Georg Holz, for whom all narrative prose was ultimately rooted in history.[25] The Dane Gudmund Schütte expressed the view that a poetic figure may, in fact, be based on several historical figures, and that, in the case of Siegfried, the "primary" historical model had been Sigibert of Austrasia, while the East Goth Uraja had served as a "secondary source" for the depiction of the hero.[26] The "Merovingian thesis" was revived after World War II by Hugo Kuhn,[27] while Helmut de Boor has pointed to the first third of the fifth century, the height of the middle Rhenish Empire of the Burgundians, as the historical platform for the later poem.[28] Finally, Otto Höfler has suggested that Siegfried is indeed the embodiment of the historical Hermann of the Cheruscans, although his interpretation of the figure is not designed to advocate the primacy of history as a key to the understanding of the *Nibelungenlied*.[29]

The mythical approach to an interpretation of the *Nibelungenlied* dominated research in the nineteenth century. The incentive had been provided by the interest in myth evinced by leading romanticists such as Friedrich Wilhelm Schelling and Georg Friedrich Creuzer. In his *Einleitung in das Nibelungen-Lied* (Introduction to the Nibelungenlied, 1818), Franz Joseph Mone claimed that the epic was actually myth that had been given poetic form. Although eighteen years later Mone was to emphasize the importance of history as the basis of the work, he now identified Siegfried with a god of light or of the sun, murdered by an enemy of the gods. He was, in essence, an old sun god of the Teutons, identical with Wodan. Friedrich Heinrich von der Hagen, who also recognized the value of the historical approach, compared Siegfried with the German deity Balder, and maintained that the *Nibelungenlied* was essentially a myth of life, death, and reincarnation.[30] Karl Lachmann, who at first had expressed reservations about the mythological interpretation of the epic, intimated to Wilhelm Grimm in a letter of 17 June 1820 his belief that, basically, the *Nibelungenlied,* or at least the first half of the work, was mythical, even if its original meaning had been lost. Wilhelm Müller identified Siegfried with the deity Freyr in his *Versuch einer mythologischen Erklärung der Nibelungensage* (Toward a mythological interpretation of the Nibelungen saga, 1841), and placed considerable emphasis on the significance of the adventures of young Siegfried as described by Hagen in the third *Aventiure.* Barend Symonds, writing in Paul's *Grundriss der germanischen Philologie,* declared that while Siegfried could not be considered the apotheosis of a god, the "Siegfried section" of the epic was rooted in myth.

The interpretation of the *Nibelungenlied* as the reflection of myth has lost ground in the twentieth century, largely owing to the influence of Heusler and Schneider and the rejection of the "methodology" of comparison advocated by its proponents. Many of the latter were contemporaries of Richard Wagner, whose influence on literary scholarship in the late nineteenth century can scarcely be overestimated. For Wagner, however, the mythical components of the *Edda* and the *Völsunga Saga* were of greater significance than the Middle High German poem. In the twentieth century, strong support for a mythical interpretation of the *Nibelungenlied* has come primarily from Otto Höfler, Franz Rolf Schröder, and Jan de Vries. Their attempts to link the fictional Siegfried to myth (in Höfler's case, also to the historical figure of Hermann) have encountered considerable resistance. Yet, while it is extremely difficult, if not impossible, to establish a definitive relationship or link between the two spheres, the contributions of Höfler, Schröder, and de Vries merit study. They do not simply represent the "rejuvenation" of romanticist speculation (although Schröder, in particular, has been generous in his praise of what he considers to be the insight demonstrated by the romanticists into the background of heroic epic). There are patterns of behavior exhibited by prominent characters in the *Nibelungenlied* which may reflect the actions of archetypal models. While one must be prudent when drawing conclusions regarding their significance for the work as a whole, the mythical, historical, and fairy-tale components are certainly there, and their explanation may easily be hindered by outright rejection of the validity of extraliterary criteria as a means for arriving at a more complete interpretation of the poem.

Myth and history have emerged as the two most significant spheres from which scholars have sought to derive the *Nibelungenlied*. At the turn of the twentieth century, Wilhelm Mundt published his ten-volume *Völkerpsychologie* (Cultural psychology), in which he claimed that heroic epic had developed from fairy tale, and that Siegfried himself was the epitome of the fairy-tale hero. This hypothesis received its keenest support from Friedrich Panzer, who believed that the events surrounding Siegfried's life and death were not to be traced back to a single fairy tale, but rather had been formulated in a series of separate tales. The *Nibelungenlied,* he claimed, had originated from a Russian fairy tale about a wooing expedition.[31] Panzer's theory has also come in for heavy criticism, largely as a result of his methodology. Werner Hoffmann has maintained that Panzer was actually comparing "abstractly formulated plot structures, which do indeed seem to agree with one another,"[32] but that these same structures have very little in common once they are subjected to rigorous textual analysis.

These, then, are the principal directions taken by scholars over the past two centuries in their attempts to discover the origins of the *Nibelungenlied*. Interest in determining the roots of the epic has waned considerably in the twentieth century, particularly since the end of World War II. This is not to imply that scholars no longer consider the issue of the *Nibelungenlied*'s genesis relevant, but rather that with the lack of more source material than is currently at our disposal, there is little opportunity to develop a sound methodology in this line of inquiry which will both elicit the support of experts and offer the promise of less speculative conclusions. To date, historical and mythical interpretations of the *Nibelungenlied* have relied heavily on the comparison of motifs, external characteristics of major figures, as well as events, in an effort to *identify* the poem with extraliterary precursors. This has led inevitably to a plethora of identifications, all of which, on the surface, may appear quite convincing, but which, for precisely this reason, mutually exclude one another from any claim to definitiveness.

A major focus of *Nibelungenlied* scholarship in this century, one which was largely neglected in the nineteenth, is the examination or interpretation of the poem in its own right, as a formidable work of art occasioned by the particular historical and social situation prevailing in Germany at the turn of the thirteenth century. Attention has been accorded the question of Siegfried's guilt, the role of legality, honor, revenge, and injustice, as well as the matter of *leit* ("sorrow"). Scholars have argued over the significance of Christianity in the work, and there have been some (for example, Goethe) who have asserted that the *Nibelungenlied* is totally heathen in nature. The dichotomy between "courtly" elements and precourtly, heroic "spirit" has come under investigation, as has the question of "individual" versus "type" figures. Psychological profiles of Siegfried, Gunther, Hagen, Kriemhild, and Brünhild, as well as other figures in the poem, have appeared, often as speculative in nature as the interpretations of scholars seeking to link the *Nibelungenlied* directly to mythology or history.

One of the delights of this masterpiece of the Staufian period is that the controversies which have arisen over the years with regard to its interpretation have done nothing to dampen the enthusiasm with which it is approached. On the contrary, even in recent times, excellent studies on the subject, in the form of books, monographs, and articles, have appeared. The reader is directed especially to the work of Gottfried Weber, Bert Nagel, Werner Hoffmann, and Walter Falk (see bibliography) among Germanists in Europe. British, American, and Canadian scholars have also been active in *Nibelungenlied* research. Regrettably, however, most of the studies undertaken outside of Germany, although of unquestionable value for scholarship, have been of a more limited nature.

Inspired by the research of Milman Parry and Albert B. Lord,[33] and the success of Francis P. Magoun, Jr., in demonstrating that oral formulism was employed by Anglo-Saxon poets as a method of composition,[34] scholars have recently considered the possibility that the *Nibelungenlied* may have been transmitted orally before having been written down. Already in his *Beiträge zur Handschriftenkritik des Nibelungenliedes,* Helmut Brackert (see note 3) had suggested that this might be the case, and the subject has continued to arouse interest and generate controversy. The leading proponent of this approach is Franz H. Bäuml, who, together with several of his colleagues and students, has strongly advocated the theory that the *Nibelungenlied*'s origins are to be sought in oral tradition.[35] Edward R. Haymes also supports this approach, although he has taken issue with the basic premise that oral poetry consists of formulaic expression while "lettered" poetry is not of a formulaic nature.[36] The reader should note Michael Curschmann's sober and critical remarks on the state of oral-formulaic research: "It is only regrettable that even the latest publications on the subject are so uncritical of their own methodology, which has, for the most part, been inherited. . . ."[37]

In the present study, I have attempted to let the *Nibelungenlied* speak for itself as much as possible. I am quite aware, of course, that the work was not composed in a vacuum, and so I have supplemented the chronological table with an overview of the cultural situation in Germany about the turn of the thirteenth century. In my discussion of the text itself, I have used the Bartsch/de Boor/ Wisniewski edition of manuscript B.[38]

Apart from an analysis of the major figures in the *Nibelungenlied,* its structure, and its language, I have tried to convey, as concisely as possible, how the *Nibelungenlied* has been received in Germany from the time of *Die Klage* to the present. That chapter does not purport to be exhaustive. Hebbel's treatment of *Die Nibelungen,* for example, could easily merit an entire book. In my concluding remarks, I have given thought to some of the major problems which continue to dominate in interpretations of the poem, but I have tried to avoid dogmatic conclusions aimed at discrediting previous views. This book is not intended as a polemic, but rather as an introduction to a great epic. I have learned much from those scholars

with whose views I take issue, as well as from those whose interpretations and analyses run close, if not necessarily parallel, to my
own.

There is considerable spatial restraint incumbent upon an author
writing for this series; I am fully aware that much more could, and
should, be said about the individual questions I have raised. Among
other things, I should emphasize that this is primarily a book about
the *Nibelungenlied*, not the *Nibelungen* tradition. I have considered
it prudent to offer my readers a basic overview of the Nordic
analogues in an appendix, but I have refrained from any detailed or
systematic treatment of these analogues. I shall make no attempt
to unravel the genealogical development of the epic, nor will I take
issue with the generally accepted assumption that the work was
composed sometime between 1198 and 1204, although I concede
that Gerhard Eis and Emil Ploss may be quite correct in maintaining
that the entire epic was already in its "final" form before 1200.[39]
It is impossible to state with certainty whether the author was a
cleric, in the medieval sense, or a knight. I share the skepticism
voiced by others that he could have been either a priest or a *Spielmann*.
It seems likely that he was at least known to, if not in the service
of, Wolfger, bishop of Passau.

While I acknowledge the historical, mythical, and fairy-tale components of the *Nibelungenlied*, I have not endeavored to "identify"
the poem as a whole or specific characters therein with extraliterary
models. Rather, I have tried to keep in mind a point well taken by
Walter Falk, namely, that the *Nibelungenlied* depicts "the aims and
misfortunes of knights and ladies, of kings and their followers," at
the turn of the thirteenth century, a "memorial to a time that was
both great and ill-fated, [a] powerful monument to a magnificent
epoch."[40]

# Chronology

1198    Otto of Brunswick elected emperor on 12 July in
        Aachen (Aix-la-Chapelle). Philip of Swabia (Hohen-
        staufen) elected emperor on 15 September in Mainz.
        Throughout this period, increase in power of indi-
        vidual princes and the pope.

ca. 1200    *Nibelungenlied* written down in form known to us.

1201    Innocent III publicly endorses Otto of Brunswick and
        excommunicates Philip.

1202–1204    Fourth Crusade.

1206    Otto defeated by Philip in Battle of Wassenberg near
        Cologne.

1208    Philip murdered by Count Otto von Wittelsbach.

1209    Otto of Brunswick crowned emperor.

1211    Frederick II (grandson of Barbarossa) succeeds Otto
        as emperor.

ca. 1240    Appearance of *Kudrun,* a post-*Nibelungenlied* epic, con-
        sidered by some scholars to be an "answer" to the
        latter.

# Chapter One
# Cultural Background

The *Nibelungenlied*, in the form in which it has been passed down to us, is a product of the Middle High German *Blütezeit*, a period of profound creativity in the history of German literature, concentrated within the years 1170 to 1250. Arthurian romance, which had flourished in France under the influence of Chrétien de Troyes, found new expression in Germany in the works of Hartmann von Aue *(Erec, Iwein)*, and in the *Parzival* of Wolfram von Eschenbach. In his *Tristan und Isolt*, based on a work by Thomas of Brittany, Gottfried von Strassburg was less concerned with upholding courtly convention than with making an appeal to what he termed the "edele herze," the "noble heart," willing to accept both joy and sorrow in its affirmation of love as an absolute. The first rendering into Middle High German of a classical theme, in conformity with medieval ideals, was undertaken by Heinrich von Veldeke in his *Eneit*, based on the French *Roman d'Enéas*, although von Veldeke was acquainted with Virgil.

The *Blütezeit* is not only the time of great courtly romances, but also of secular lyrics, specifically, *Minnesang*, the love poetry of the nobility. Its foremost representatives include Heinrich von Veldeke, Friedrich von Hausen, Reinmar der Alte, Hartmann von Aue, Walther von der Vogelweide, Heinrich von Morungen, and Albrecht von Johannsdorf.

The *Nibelungenlied*, written about the turn of the thirteenth century, is unique. Its very existence begs a question that continues to occupy scholars: what was the function of an heroic epic which obviously enjoyed considerable popularity among a ruling class whose ideals of moderation *(mâze)*, consistency *(staete)*, loyalty *(triuwe)*, and honor *(êre)* seemed to find perfect expression in Arthurian romance?[1] In the *Nibelungenlied* there is none of the customary optimism associated with courtly romance. Injustice and calamity are not resolved in the ultimate reconciliation of hostile forces or in the development of an individual self-awareness and understanding of one's place within the order of things, culminating in the betterment

1

of society as a whole (compare *Parzival*). Transgressions and conflict
in the epic lead, with what one might describe as unrelenting
necessity, to greater catastrophes and the eventual demise of two
great peoples. And yet the ideals which are so much a component
of the literature of the day are by no means absent in the *Nibelungenlied*. Paradoxically, the actions taken by the Burgundians while
defending themselves against the Huns epitomize some of these very
ideals, namely, *triuwe, êre,* and *staete.*

We shall have occasion to return to the question of the *Nibelungenlied* within a literary world accustomed to "happy endings" and the
resolution of difficulties or antagonisms. Prior to doing so, however,
we shall acquaint ourselves with the world and time in which the
epic came into being and flourished.

Politically, it was a time of unrest, as indicated in the Chronology.
Although Barbarossa had aspired to bring about imperial unity, his
efforts can hardly be termed a success, and after his death the power
of the territorial princes increased considerably. Political stability
was lacking, and subsequent candidates for the imperial throne
demonstrated little of the character, resolve, or means upon which
the idea of universal empire was predicated. Franz Bäuml has contended that "the *Nibelungenlied* testifies to the clash of the highly
developed Hohenstaufen state with its competitors for legitimacy,
and the dangers this confrontation held for the fabric of German
society."[2] This is, of course, a highly speculative theory concerning
the poet's motives for writing down the epic. While it is hardly
conceivable that he was ignorant of the political events transpiring
around him, our poet seems less concerned with offering a portrait
of the Staufian (and hence imperial) predicament, than he is with
presenting a tale about individual heroes and heroines, their virtues
and vices, and, of course, the terrible consequences both for themselves and for entire peoples which stem from their imprudent actions.

The *Nibelungenlied* has often been referred to as a "Volksepos," a
"folk epic." Insofar as this is meant to imply participation of the
"folk" (in a broad sense) in the creative process, or even in its
enjoyment as listeners or readers, the term is a misnomer. For
whether the *Nibelungenlied* was written by a knight or a cleric, we
can be sure that it was conceived as *Standesdichtung,* that is, poetry
written or recited for a particular class of society, and that the class
in question would not have been any other than that of the nobility,
the *Ritter* of the late twelfth century.[3] This was not simply a warrior

class. While the nobles did indeed spend much of their lives either training for or participating in wars or feuds, their originally fierce individualism was tempered by the spread of Christianity. To the warrior's courage, his love of adventure, his honor and loyalty to the liege lord, were now added compassion toward those in need, mercy toward the vanquished enemy, and resolve to do battle for Christ and church. The pivotal ideal, at least in theory, was that of moderation *(mâze)*.

Becoming a knight was a three-stage affair. The aspirant first served as a page at court, where he was taught good manners, how to ride, hunt, hawk and, above all, fight. The spear, sword, and the battle-ax were the weapons in whose use the aspirant was expected to become proficient. But the page also learned how to distinguish different knights and noble houses, and this involved a knowledge of shields and coats of arms. Heraldry was a basic component of the curriculum. Once he had completed this first part of his training, the page became a squire to a knight and was charged with responsibility for the latter's shield and armor. As a knight's attendant, the squire was constantly exposed to the various spheres of the world into which he expected to be initiated: the court, tournaments, jousts, feuds, battle. He became intimately acquainted with the conventions associated with knighthood: how to behave in the company of one's peers and superiors, the significance of proper attire, the obligations owed to those higher on the social scale, as well as to the church.

In order to advance to knighthood, the aspirant could be expected to perform some deed of arms to prove his worth. The initiation itself was a regal affair during which the squire knelt before his lord and received the accolade (a hard blow on the neck with the flat of a sword). In Germany, the squire was initiated through the *Schwertumgürtung,* the "belting-on" of the knight's sword. A mass was heard before the actual knighting and, subsequent to it, a vigil observed over the knight's arms in a church. On occasion, the knighting was performed by a bishop. As an example of the significance of this act and the festive atmosphere which it engendered, the reader is directed to strophes 29–33 of the *Nibelungenlied,* which depict the knighting of Siegfried.

Once knighted, the noble became a member of a privileged society, and it is evident that the knights were conscious of belonging to an elite. This awareness of their particular status was reinforced

when representatives of the nobility from numerous European coun-
tries served together in a common cause during the crusades. The
realization that they were unique found expression in the glorification and idealization of their class and their views of life in the
Arthurian literature of the High Middle Ages. Becoming a knight
brought with it considerable obligations, of course. The former
aspirant had been initiated into adult society and had become a
member of a select fighting class. His initiation was predicated upon
the belief in an ordered society in which his behavior as a noble
could be expected to constitute a model for others.

I have already alluded to the ideals of this military class, which
found their finest expression in the courtly romances and lyric poetry
of the Golden Age of Middle High German literature. The world
of the knight was that of the court, beautiful women, challenging
adventures, magnificent festivals, and the ever-present dichotomy
between joy and sorrow.

Walther von der Vogelweide, Hartmann von Aue, Wolfram von
Eschenbach, and Heinrich von Veldeke were themselves knights.
Two concepts figure prominently in their works: *gotes hulde* ("God's
grace") and *der werlt hulde* ("the respect and recognition of one's
fellow knights"). The question arose as to how both goals could be
attained in this world, and this became one of the major themes of
courtly literature at the close of the twelfth century.[4]

Caution must be exercised, however, when attempting to ascertain
the relationship between the poetic expression of such ideals and
reality. Was the knight actually bound by a "system of virtues?"
Are the Middle High German romances essentially a reflection of
reality in the late twelfth and early thirteenth centuries? In brief,
are the poetic masterpieces historical documents from which scholars
can derive an accurate portrait of medieval German knighthood?
These and similar questions form the nucleus of an on-going controversy in the scholarly community.[5] Erich Auerbach's remarks
concerning idealization in Chrétien de Troyes's *Yvain* bear keeping
in mind:

Such idealization takes us very far from the imitation of reality. In the
courtly romance the functional, the historically real aspects of class are
passed over. Though it offers a great many culturally significant details
concerning the customs of social intercourse and external social forms and
conventions in general, we can get no penetrating view of contemporary

reality from it, even in respect to the knightly class. Where it depicts reality, it depicts merely the colorful surface, and where it is not superficial, it has other subjects and other ends than contemporary reality. Yet it does contain a class ethics which as such claimed and indeed attained acceptance and validity in this real and earthly world. For it has a great power of attraction which, if I mistake not, is due especially to two characteristics which distinguish it: it is absolute, raised above all earthly contingencies, and it gives those who submit to its dictates the feeling that they belong to a community of the elect, a circle of solidarity (the term comes from Hellmut Ritter, the Orientalist) set apart from the common herd. The ethics of feudalism, the ideal conception of the perfect knight, thus attained a very considerable and very long-lived influence.[6]

The medieval knight has been described as "a bundle of para-doxes—a romantic lover and a libertine, a gallant knight and a bloodthirsty brute, a devout Christian and a flouter of the elements of morality."[7] His relationship to other members of society could be quite ambivalent. On the surface, the knights of Germany in the High Middle Ages were Christians, although it was not un-common for an ecclesiastical and a lay baron to find themselves at odds over secular matters, for example, the claim to land or, for that matter, the favor of a particular woman. In an area where one might have expected much more mutual antagonism, that of the knight's inherent bellicosity, we find that the aims of both parties often tended to coincide. From the time of St. Augustine, the church had compromised on its original condemnation of all killing. While it made every effort to discourage indiscriminate violence, partic-ularly among the nobles themselves, it accepted killing "in the name of God." The crusades provide ample evidence of the position assumed by the church in this respect. But it had little support to offer for tournaments or jousts, and here it was not alone. Criticism of knights and their behavior emanated from several quarters in the second half of the twelfth century. At issue was not the warrior character of the nobility, but rather the incredible amount of time wasted in senseless, and often self-destructive, feuding, immoderate living, and the general predominance of self-interest as the basic motive for all their actions. Subtle criticism of knightly ways may be detected in the works of Hartmann von Aue and Gottfried von Strassburg, but there is little to compare with the scathing com-mentary on the subject by the English philosopher John of Salisbury in the sixth book of his *Policraticus*. Those who do not meet John's rigorous standards are, in his opinion, false knights, and should not be tolerated among the assembly of the elite. As with the clergy, the knights are a consecrated sect, the principal defenders of the church and the state.[8]

The relationship of the knight to women was as ambiguous as his relationship to the church and the teachings of Christianity. On the one hand, we find the medieval woman of high social standing revered to the point of idealization. The romances and lyric poetry abound with hyperbolic praise of fine women; jousts and tournaments, as well as the inevitable adventures, would lose much of their significance without the opportunity afforded the knight to impress a woman of the court, perhaps even to acquire her favor. In some instances, the poetry of the High Middle Ages leaves us with the impression that there existed a veritable cult of womanhood that inspired knights to new heights of personal endeavor and achievement. On the other hand, the chronicles of the period paint a somewhat less favorable picture of the relationship between the two sexes. Reports of brutal floggings of wives by their "noble" husbands—a practice condoned by canon law—were not uncommon; nor, for that matter, were divorces, even though they were condemned by the church. In contrast to her idealized portrayal in literature, a woman's position in society was ultimately determined by her sex, not her individuality. She was subordinated to man, at least in the view of the church and in the eyes of the judicial system. It is hardly surprising that we possess little indication that women figured significantly in the "cultural" processes of that epoch: "Literary works by women are rare, apart from the love letters of Heloïse or the outpourings of great women mystics and a few writings of learned nuns."[9] The position of woman in medieval society is inherently paradoxical: she is, at one and the same time, the seducer of mankind (Eve) and its redeemer (Mary). Woman holds a specific place within the *ordo* of things, and this place is determined by her inferiority to man, a doctrine propagated by the church and supported wholeheartedly by the aristocracy, a view still poignantly expressed by Katharina in her final speech in act 5 of Shakespeare's *Taming of the Shrew.*

In contrast to the relatively passive role of many women in Arthurian romance, we shall see that the female protagonists in the *Nibelungenlied* are vital, active figures. Neither Kriemhild nor Brünhild remains within the mold described above. While Kriemhild would appear to conform to the image of the dependent princess prior to her marriage to Siegfried and may, in one instance, furnish us with an example of the "battered wife," her behavior subsequent to the murder of her husband illustrates that she is not simply a bereaved widow, but also a character capable of transcending the *ordo* of courtly society to the point of bringing about its destruction. The wooing of Brünhild might be regarded by some as an attempt on the part of a male-dominated society to force the individualistic female who lives by her own rules into conformity with that society. Intentional disregard for the plight of the female protagonists in the *Nibelungenlied* constitutes one of the basic reasons for the catastrophe which ensues.

Some scholars have regarded the courtly romances with their models of knighthood and chivalrous behavior, their festivals and tournaments, their opulent splendor, as an escape from the reality of an otherwise boring and manifestly uncomfortable existence.[10] The actual relationship between the fictional world and the real court may be immensely difficult, if not impossible, to ascertain. If we are unable, however, to establish a definitive parallel between these two spheres, it is not unreasonable to assume that the ideals depicted in courtly literature reflected, at least to some degree, the aspirations of the nobility. In the *Nibelungenlied,* adherence to such ideals does not preserve society. In the following pages, we shall examine the manner in which absolutism replaces *mâze,* ultimately bringing society to its knees.

Prior to turning our attention to the *Nibelungenlied* itself, we must consider the question of literary patronage. In a recent book on the subject, Joachim Bumke has stated that "medieval art was art that was commissioned, and must be considered as such."[11] This is particularly true of the great courtly romances, and it was undoubtedly the case for the *Nibelungenlied.* There were, after all, no publishers or copyright in the twelfth century. A knight-poet relied on the favor of wealthy patrons. His fate, at least as an author, was intimately bound to the welfare, and often whims, of his benefactor. Bumke suggests that the considerable number of "literary torsos" from the *Blütezeit* may be an indication of support withdrawn by a patron. A crucial problem confronting the scholar of medieval literary patronage is the lack of convincing evidence to link an author with a specific benefactor. The chronicles of the period are of no assistance in this regard; in the final analysis, the literary texts themselves must be consulted. Often enough, these, too, give scant evidence of individual relationships. We do not know, for example, who the patrons of Hartmann von Aue, Wolfram von Eschenbach, or Gottfried von Strassburg may have been, but it would be imprudent to suggest that the works which they wrote were uncommissioned.

In the case of the *Nibelungenlied,* the question of patronage is further complicated by the fact that the author has remained anonymous. The most widely embraced theory is that the work was probably commissioned by Wolfger of Erla, bishop of Passau between 1191 and 1204, and patron of Walther von der Vogelweide.[12] It has also been suggested that the Babenberg Duke Henry II Jasomirgott, who died in 1177, might have been the patron of the author of the hypothetical forerunner of the *Nibelungenlied,* the *Ältere Not.*[13] Few have accepted this theory, however, and Willy Krogmann's suggestion that Duke Berthold IV of Zähringen could have been the poet's benefactor[14] has likewise been greeted with skepticism.

George F. Jones has maintained that "there is no reason to deny that Austria's greatest medieval lyric poet [Walther von der Vogelweide] could have written Austria's greatest contemporary epic." Jones assures his readers that his study "does not conclude that Walther composed the *Nibelungenlied,*"[15] but claiming that there is no reason to believe he could not have done so does not bring us closer to a determination of the actual authorship of the poem. The latest contribution on the authorship of the *Nibelungenlied* by Berta Lösel-Wieland-Engelmann, "Verdanken wir das Nibelungenlied einer Niedernburger Nonne?"[16] is highly speculative and equally problematical.

The matter of patronage and authorship of the *Nibelungenlied* may well remain one of the unanswerable questions surrounding the work without the addition of more secondary material than we currently possess. I would concur with Bumke that the *Nibelungenlied* was, in all likelihood, the work of a *clericus,*[17] but any attempt to identify this person more specifically on the basis of available information is an exercise in futility.

We have alluded above to the question of the function of the *Nibelungenlied* in Germany at a time when courtly romance predominated. The poem abounds with courtly elements (Siegfried's knighting, the initial description of Kriemhild, the *Minne*-relationship between Siegfried and Kriemhild, and the attention accorded the description of fine clothes, gems, and festivals),[18] but these cannot temper the "absolute" spirit of the epic, which stands in marked contrast to the plea for moderation so evident in the Arthurian romances. Was the *Nibelungenlied* an attempt to demonstrate, in the most vivid manner imaginable, the consequences to be faced by a society which turned its back on moderation? If this is indeed the case, it would be imprudent to suggest that the author necessarily intended to view such a process in moral terms. I do not believe that the text provides us with evidence to support such a hypothesis, nor would I subscribe to the theory that disregard for Christian mores and the concept of the divine *ordo* was considered implicitly as a prime cause for the catastrophe suffered by the Burgundians and Huns at the conclusion of the work. Rather, it seems to me that the absence of a resounding and uncompromising condemnation of acts perpetrated by individuals and peoples alike may be considered an indication of the possibility that the author accepted the course of events as inevitable and unalterable. In so doing, he would have represented a striking contrast to virtually all of his contemporaries in the literary sphere. Our poet was clearly of another mold than the author of *Erec* and *Iwein,* of *Tristan,* or of *Parzival.* The spirit of the *Nibelungenlied* betrays an acceptance of the tragic concept of life.[19] The author was, perhaps, as Hebbel has suggested, a dramatist through and through, but he was no moralist. It was not his intention to suggest that this view of life be overcome or superseded by another, one more in conformity with the ideals, and dogma, of Christianity and chivalry. He acknowledges both, but his interest lies quite clearly in the portrayal of figures who both generate and epitomize a tragic existence, one in which the poet himself appears to acquiesce.

## Chapter Two
# The Major Figures

## Kriemhild

It would not be an exaggeration to claim that the *Nibelungenlied* is, in essence, the story of Kriemhild. She is with us from beginning to end, the first figure introduced by name in the epic, and the last to perish in the slaughter of Burgundians and Huns at its conclusion. Kriemhild is a woman of considerable complexity. Described as "ein vil edel magedîn" ("a most noble maiden") in the second strophe of the work, her beauty is almost simultaneously linked to future calamity: "si wart ein scoene wîp. / dar umbe muosen degene      vil verliesen den lîp" ("She was a beautiful woman and, as a result, many a knight was later to lose his life," 2.3–4). The basic dichotomy inherent in the poem is already in evidence in the delineation of Kriemhild: joy and sorrow are inseparable.

It would be inaccurate to maintain that Kriemhild undergoes a radical metamorphosis from beautiful queen in the first half of the *Nibelungenlied* to a degenerate *vâlandinne* ("She-devil") by its conclusion. The transformation is gradual, her road into total depravity lined with many a sign for the observant reader that we are dealing here with someone whose potential for destruction is early documented. Her reaction to Ute's interpretation of the dream, in which a falcon reared by Kriemhild is torn asunder by two eagles, exemplifies her basic tendency to absolutize. Her decision to reject any suitors, to withdraw from any active participation in the wooing ritual (18), represents a rejection of the two poles which prevail in the world: joy and sorrow. Kriemhild's attitude is entirely self-centered, and her decision to effect an absolute withdrawal from the sphere in which she could be expected to function, namely, as an eligible bride-to-be awaiting the appropriate suitor, illustrates that she is much more than a beautiful Burgundian princess. The key word here is "absolute." Gottfried Weber attributes already at this point a high degree of awareness on the part of Kriemhild that an untimely end to a love born of *total* commitment can only lead to

10

total ruin.[1] Her reaction to the interpretation of the dream is symptomatic of her egocentricity, her lack of flexibility when faced with a potential or real crisis. It is also the first indication we have of Kriemhild's inclination to isolate herself from the court, a tendency which later, carried to the extreme, will place her in direct and fatal confrontation with the latter.

Lest we be accused of having painted, at the outset, a far too negative picture of Kriemhild, let the reader be assured that we do not intend to suggest that the Burgundian princess is without merit. In strophe 3, she is depicted as the epitome of the courtly ideal of womanhood, "minneclîch" ("lovable"), "âne mâzen schoene" ("beautiful beyond measure"), and endowed with "tugende" ("exemplary character traits") which make her the honor of her sex. When Siegfried later appears at Worms, we discover that Kriemhild is indeed capable of love, although it is unlikely that this is the sole reason that she is attracted to the hero of Xanten. It is important to note, however, that the darker side of Kriemhild is in evidence from the beginning of the epic.

The impression gained of Kriemhild's attraction to Siegfried is not tempered by any suspicion that the Burgundian princess has an ulterior motive in selecting him as her escort for the festival, subsequent to his successful campaign against the Saxons and Danes. The "knowing" and secret exchange of glances between the two— "mit lieben ougen blicken    ein ander sâhen an" (293.3)—is indicative of *Minnesang*-convention. Her love is genuine, as is his. But it is also significant that Kriemhild had earlier inquired of a messenger not how Siegfried had fared in the struggle, but rather who had acquitted himself best on the battlefield (226.3); and the news that Siegfried had turned out to be the hero of the day, with no one else so much as approximating his achievements, is greeted with unmistakable delight: "ir kunden disiu maere    nimmer lieber gesîn" ("She could not have received more joyful news," 238.4). For Kriemhild, then, the attraction to Siegfried is not based solely on spontaneous love, but rather her love is rooted, to a considerable degree, in the stature and fame enjoyed by Siegfried. These two components, love and power, are integral to her relationship to Siegfried. Marriage to the most powerful man in the world brings with it increased honor and prestige.

By themselves, the honor, power, and prestige which Kriemhild acquires through her marriage to Siegfried are positive factors. What is problematic is Kriemhild's repeated need to assert her position (as well as that of her husband) in a manner which cannot fail to provoke antagonism from her own clan. Her insistence in 691.1–3 that she be accorded certain Burgundian territories prior to her departure for Xanten provides a clear indication of her awareness of the significance which material goods and possessions convey within society. Had she been content to accept Siegfried's rebuff that she can well do without her inheritance (which the Burgundians were quite willing to grant her), Kriemhild might simply have been judged, at least at this point, as the epitome of the protocol-conscious spouse, a figure who would have much in common with her counterparts in the Arthurian romances of the period. She presses the issue, however, and declares that while Siegfried may reject her inheritance, it will not be so easy to dispose of the Burgundian knights whom she wishes to take back with her to Xanten, for "si müg' ein künic gerne    füeren in sîn lant" ("A king would be happy to have them accompany him to his kingdom," 696.3). The fact that she sends for Hagen and Ortwin, the best among the Burgundian warriors, is testimony not only to her self-importance, but also to her lack of discretion and sensitivity toward the traditions of her own people. Hagen is as integral to Worms and the Burgundian dynasty as Gunther himself; more than a chief counselor, he is a type of permanent bodyguard, a man whose fate is ultimately linked to that of Worms and to whom separation from the royal family is unthinkable. Judging by his angry response to the suggestion that he accompany Kriemhild and Siegfried to Xanten (698–99), it is apparent that Kriemhild has committed more than a simple faux pas. By defying a basic and obviously long-standing tradition among the Burgundians, she has evinced a degree of alienation from her family and the court at Worms which is destined to become decidedly more pronounced as the epic progresses. But just as important as Kriemhild's claims to land and vassals—as justified or unwarranted as these may be—is the fact that the queen is soundly rebuffed, first by her husband, and then by Hagen. To one as self-conscious of her position as Kriemhild, this cannot help but sting, and it is only the first in a series of instances in which she is forced to comply with the decisions of the men around her, suffering, on later occasions, even greater affronts to her honor and pride.

We may state with considerable justification that with her marriage to Siegfried, Kriemhild has entered into another sphere of existence, and that she has, for all intents and purposes, turned her back on Worms and its interests. Having become the wife of the most powerful man in the world, she acquires a heightened awareness of her own importance, and nowhere is this more apparent than in her dispute with Brünhild in the fourteenth *Aventiure*. Friedrich Maurer has claimed that the quarrel between the two queens begins in a "quite harmless way,"[2] when Kriemhild praises Siegfried in a somewhat immoderate fashion in Brünhild's presence. However, the manner in which Kriemhild is caught up in a veritable ecstasy of admiration for Siegfried, comparing him to the moon while the other knights are merely stars (817), is really anything but harmless. At this point, her words may not be deliberately chosen to hurt Brünhild or to call into question the stature of Worms or of her brother, but they are quite indicative of her extreme lack of tact and her penchant for *superbia*. Moreover, she is uttering them in the presence of a woman who, despite some nagging doubts about the way things may seem, could well imagine herself to be wed to the more powerful man, the only one, in fact, capable of besting her in public tests of strength as well as in the bedroom, namely, Gunther. Besides, as Siegfried has declared himself to be a liegeman of Gunther's, claims such as those made by Kriemhild, that, for example, all of these (presumably Burgundian) lands could well be ruled over by her husband (815.3-4), can only be regarded as both arrogant and preposterous. One might well ask: just how much does Kriemhild know about the deceit practiced by Siegfried and Gunther toward Brünhild? As she is in possession of the latter's ring and girdle, we can assume that Siegfried told her at least something of the circumstances by which he acquired them. It is not unlikely that he informed Kriemhild of the "service" performed by him for Gunther in the latter's nuptial quarters, although he may well have left much to Kriemhild's imagination in the process. Regardless of just how well informed Kriemhild may be, she is cognizant of the fact that her husband is a "better" or greater man than her brother in purely human terms, and that he is certainly Gunther's equal in a social respect: "geloubestu des, Prünhilt,    er ist wol Gunthers genôz" ("Believe me, Brünhild, he is certainly equal to Gunther," 819.4). The idea that Siegfried could be anyone's liegeman is anathema to Kriemhild (note 822).

It appears that Kriemhild is incapable of recognizing the imprudence of her words at this juncture. The relatively positive relationship that prevails between the Burgundians and Siegfried rests on the preservation of a myth, namely, that of Gunther's "superiority." Were this myth to be destroyed, the reputation of both Gunther and the court of Worms could well be compromised beyond repair. By allowing *passio* to dominate *ratio* in this scene, Kriemhild almost gives away the secret upon which the relationship between her husband and the Burgundians rests. It is impossible to separate the genuine concern felt by Kriemhild to uphold the position of Siegfried from a less selfless desire to· preserve her own image. Her egocentricity is particularly in evidence when she deliberately turns the argument into a full-fledged power struggle by declaring—in the presence of two Burgundian warriors—that she will put it to the test and see whether she can enter the cathedral before Brünhild. To this, A. T. Hatto comments: "Kriemhild's language is reminiscent of set challenges between heroes of the older period, and it is to be noted that the presence of the warriors, which she invokes, will give her 'duel' with Brunhild a quasi juridical status."[3] Kriemhild is not content to declare that Siegfried is of "higher standing" (note 828.2: "tiwerr") than Gunther: "ich wil selbe wesen tiwerr,     danne iemen habe bekant / deheine küneginne,     diu krône ie her getruoc" ("I myself claim to be superior to any Queen who has ever worn a crown!" 829.2–3).

The blatant *superbia* displayed by Kriemhild in this scene is indicative of her tendency to absolutize, to give full reign to her egocentricity. She outdoes Siegfried in her brashness; he may claim upon his arrival at Worms that he intends to wrest all of Gunther's lands and peoples from him, but at no time does he proclaim publicly that these are his due because he is greater than anyone who has ever lived. By now, the more positive attributes associated with Kriemhild at the commencement of the poem have become completely overshadowed by her arrogance. Even if she is not fully aware of the nature of Siegfried's assistance to Gunther, she knows in her heart that her husband is, in fact, the "better" man and that, therefore, she is the better woman. This might be regarded, at least in part, as evidence of her devotion to Siegfried; yet it is simultaneously a hard blow struck not only at Brünhild, but also, and more importantly, at Worms. The more intense the confrontation between Kriemhild and Brünhild becomes, the more alienated Kriemhild becomes from her own family, and this estrangement eventually leads to outright hostility.

The scene in front of the minster is a highpoint of the epic and shows the anonymous poet to be a gifted "dramatist." That such a lack of harmony should be demonstrated before the church is paradoxical, even more so the fact that the minster should be used as a visible testing ground of the respective power of the two queens. The order of entry into the church weighs more than the spiritual experience one expects to have inside. What contains significance is that which is on the outside, that which can be seen and which is, therefore, real, and, in this instance, a confirmation of legitimacy. It should never be forgotten that Kriemhild provokes Brünhild publicly. This display of antagonism is witnessed by any number of ladies-in-waiting and other court personnel. When Kriemhild loses her composure entirely and claims that Brünhild has brought shame upon her body by having been Siegfried's lover (839.3–4; 840.2–4), she shows herself to be devoid of any sense of propriety. Kriemhild's egotism, coupled with her inability to compromise, has produced a situation which is nothing less than catastrophic for members of her own family and, ultimately, for Siegfried and herself. As she becomes more and more a part of Siegfried's world, Kriemhild appears increasingly less bound to the mores of courtly society. Her producing of the ring and girdle which Siegfried had taken from Brünhild on her wedding night (847, 849–50) is malicious; this, too, is done in public, and what in modern judicial proceedings might be considered "circumstantial evidence" is, in the Middle Ages, irrefutable proof of the act.

It is a predominant character trait of Kriemhild either to ignore or to be unaware of the larger ramifications of her actions. Stated succinctly, she lacks wisdom. Neither in this instance, nor in the second half of the epic, does the queen reflect on the potential consequences of her words and deeds. Through her immoderate behavior, she has rapidly dispelled much of the image of the loving, beautiful bride of Siegfried, the epitome of the idealized lady of the court, creating more the impression of a determined egotist who will tolerate nothing which she views as in any way casting a shadow upon her status or that of her husband.

We have established that position and power are of paramount importance in Kriemhild's life. Yet, combined with her arrogant self-assertiveness is a dangerous naiveté. Kriemhild appears oblivious to the full extent to which she has compromised the Burgundians by revealing the secret of Brünhild's "taming." It is but further

evidence of her egocentricity that she proves incapable of putting
herself into their position. When she addresses Hagen as "[v]il lieber
vriunt" ("dear friend," 893.1), and entrusts him with Siegfried's
safety during the fatal hunt, it is clear that she continues to place
absolute trust in familial relationships.[4] In this respect, Kriemhild
is similar to Siegfried. Both are capable—through word and deed—
of creating havoc within the Burgundian realm without ever realizing precisely how much damage they have done. As a Burgundian
princess, Kriemhild, through her widely acclaimed beauty, brought
honor to Worms. As Siegfried's queen, she has become dangerous
to the court. Whereas one might have expected—as undoubtedly
the Burgundians had—that such a union would bring about a formidable alliance between Burgundy and Xanten, the marriage has
actually served to widen the rift between the two, although it is
unlikely that anyone other than Hagen is fully aware that this is
the case.

The murder of Siegfried has been correctly referred to as the act
which sets the wheels of revenge in motion, causing Kriemhild to
degenerate into a veritable she-devil, and bringing about the destruction of both Burgundians and Huns. Kriemhild shares in the
moral guilt for her husband's death through her indiscretions before
the minster. Her betrayal of his vulnerable spot attests to her naiveté,
to the often apparent incongruence in Kriemhild's behavior. The
queen is capable of inflicting incredible injury, as we have witnessed
in the case of her dispute with Brünhild. She may also be portrayed
as the loving and fearful spouse, by no means unaware of the dangers
this world may hold even for Siegfried. Yet it is her inability to
reflect on the deeper significance of words and actions which stands
out here. Has Kriemhild forgotten the angry response of Hagen to
her suggestion that he accompany her back to Xanten? Can she have
been so insensitive to the seriousness with which he regards his
position at Worms and ignore the fact that Gunther's prime counselor has been both humiliated by Siegfried upon the latter's arrival
at court, and subsequently forced to assume a subordinate role in
the war against the Danes and Saxons? This naiveté, which eventually leads her to betray Siegfried, however unwittingly, into the
hands of his murderer, can be attributed to her egocentricity (her
love of and loyalty to Siegfried notwithstanding), and it is this
darker side of her personality which precludes any real understanding
on her part for the sensitivities of others. It is as though the world

existed only for the benefit of both herself and her spouse, and this mentality, in itself, poses a great threat both to society in general and the Burgundian court in particular. It is Kriemhild's self-centeredness which ultimately makes the murder of Siegfried possible. Although forewarned through two dreams of the danger facing him (921, 924), and now finally aware of the indiscretion committed by having divulged his secret to Hagen, Kriemhild fails to inform Siegfried, stating merely that she fears someone might wish him harm (922). Why does she not simply tell him that Hagen knows where he is vulnerable? Her tactlessness before the minster had earned her a sound beating from Siegfried; is it fear of how he might react to her confession which stops her from admitting her error? Yet, if we contend that the total grief later perceived by Kriemhild is born of the total love she held for her husband, how can we reconcile this with her present behavior? I believe the answers to these questions are fairly clear: Kriemhild's love of Siegfried is indisputable, but it is still a notch below her concern for herself. Put bluntly, Kriemhild is prepared to take the risk that Siegfried will never return from the hunt rather than chance the possibility of another thrashing. Stanza 920 illustrates at one and the same time how very much aware Kriemhild is that her husband is in grave danger and the extent to which she fears his wrath were she to tell him the truth:

> Do gedâhtes' an diu maere     (sine torst' ir niht gesagen),
> diu si dâ Hagenen sagete:     dô begonde klagen
> diu edel küneginne,     daz sie ie gewan den lîp.
> dô weinte âne mâze     des herren Sîfrides wîp.

(Then she thought of what she had told Hagen, but she did not dare tell him about it. The noble queen began to lament that she had ever been born. Lord Siegfried's wife wept without restraint.)

The murder of Siegfried grieves Kriemhild in at least three ways: (1) it robs her of the man with whom she is deeply in love (Siegfried as a person); (2) it deprives her of the source of much of her prestige and power (Siegfried as a status symbol); (3) it makes her acutely aware of her own guilt (1008.1–2; see also 1111–12) and of the extent to which she has allowed herself to be deceived. From this moment on, Kriemhild's sole purpose in life is to exact revenge.

One might well maintain that, structurally, the second half of the
epic revolves around Kriemhild and Hagen as antagonists, the development of individual animosities into a cataclysmic series of
events culminating in the mass destruction of Burgundians and
Huns. Of note is the fact that Kriemhild never seeks to find inner
peace; remarkably, she finds no solace in the Christian God. She
may pray for Siegfried's soul (1103.3), but this, together with the
numerous instances in which the church serves as a backdrop to her
grieving for her husband, is not indicative of a love of Christ, but
rather of her love for Siegfried.[5]

Why does Kriemhild remain in Worms, rather than accompany
her father-in-law, Siegmund, back to Xanten? Why does she, moreover, turn her back on her son by Siegfried, the young Gunther,
allowing him to return to the Netherlands with his grandfather?
Kriemhild maintains that, having no relatives in the land of the
Nibelungs, it would be better for her to remain in Worms, where
she has family to help her mourn Siegfried (1085, 1088). Although
it might be suggested that, despite her resolve not to see Hagen
(1078–79), Kriemhild is already giving thought to exacting revenge
on the latter and that this can best be realized by remaining in
Worms, there is no indication in the text at this point that this is,
in fact, the case. Kriemhild certainly desires revenge, but she has
not yet reached the point of deliberate scheming or intrigue against
Hagen. Her de facto rejection of her child, however, is highly
significant. At no time throughout the *Nibelungenlied* does the poet
make any effort to portray Kriemhild as capable of "normal" maternal instincts toward her offspring. The removal of the young
Gunther from her presence is simultaneously a sign that the queen
has given up a good part of her own humanity. Moreover, by
rejecting her son, Kriemhild has symbolically turned her back on
the concept of a productive (and consoling) future; she has, in
essence, lapsed into a type of nihilism. For the time being, she
allows herself to be consumed by grief, but later this will be augmented by her fanatic drive to have Hagen's head. The court with
all its trappings means nothing to her; the vitality is gone, and in
its place there is only the will to destroy. Kriemhild's alienation
from Worms could not have been greater had she accompanied
Siegmund back to Xanten. Hers is no mere physical isolation, but
rather a spiritual estrangement from everything for which the court
stands, and this is underscored by a four-and-a-half year self-con-

finement during which she does not even speak to her brother Gunther.

The theft of the *hort* ("treasure") inherited from Siegfried serves further to alienate Kriemhild from her family. The *hort* and Siegfried have been intimately linked to one another by Werner Schröder,[6] but of equal significance is the tremendous value of this treasure, which includes, among other things, "von golde ein rüetelîn" ("a golden rod," 1124. 1), capable of making its owner the most powerful man in the world. In Kriemhild's hands, the treasure clearly represents a threat to Worms in general and Hagen in particular. For the first time since the murder of Siegfried, Kriemhild is again in a position of power, able to attract the services of foreign knights (1127). At this point, Kriemhild has already begun to consider how she might "deal" with Hagen. A power basis is essential, since it is clear that she may well have to contend with the forces commanded by her own brothers. There is a very real threat of a devastating clash between Kriemhild's mercenaries and the Burgundians at Worms itself. Removal of the treasure is, from Hagen's point of view, the only solution.

The loss of the *hort* causes Kriemhild to lapse into yet greater isolation for eight-and-a-half years. Consumed by both sorrow and hate, she has no foreseeable opportunity of avenging the wrong done her by Hagen. Kriemhild has already begun the process of degeneration which will see her end as a demonic *vâlandinne,* a "she-devil," but it is necessary to consider how those around her have forced her into this position of isolation and, ultimately, alienation. Hagen has been able to rob her of both Siegfried and the *hort,* and while her brothers condemn both acts on the surface, no one of prominence (other than Siegmund) has emerged to support her against Hagen. The lack of any substantial assistance from Gunther, Gernot, and Giselher—an impossible expectation when one reflects on the full extent of their complicity—contributes to Kriemhild's rejection of her family and helps to set in motion the series of events which will eventually result in the extermination of the Burgundian royal clan and the larger part of its followers.

Although it is clear that Kriemhild bears much of the responsibility for the wrong done her, our sympathies lie, for the most part, with her at the conclusion of the first half of the epic. Her resolve to avenge the murder of Siegfried is both humanly understandable and legally justifiable, but the involvement of her brothers

in the deed precludes any possibility that Hagen would simply be
turned over to her. She is without any recourse whatsoever at this
point. Inner reflection might have given her cause to temper her
hatred of Hagen; instead, however, Kriemhild tends to simplify the
issue: Siegfried has been treacherously slain by Hagen with the full
knowledge of her brothers, and for that, the hero of Troneck, at
least, must pay with his life.

Kriemhild's marriage to Attila is a sham. It is not concluded by
her in order to restore harmony and productivity to a mourning
Hunnish Empire, or to acquire inner peace for herself, but solely
for the purpose of obtaining another power base. When Kriemhild
is removed from her self-imposed isolation at Worms, it is not the
first step in a process designed to reintegrate her into courtly society.
From the moment she is assured of Rüdeger's fidelity (1256) and
agrees to become Attila's wife, her image is primarily that of the
scheming, malevolent vixen. Siegfried remains paramount in her
mind, and the desire to avenge him has already become an obsession:
"waz ob noch wirt errochen  des mînen lieben mannes lîp!" (1259,4;
see also 1260).[7] When Kriemhild departs for Hungary and the court
of Attila, she is removed forever from the realm of Worms, both
physically and spiritually. In the eyes of the Huns, she may represent
the guarantee that their country will again prosper, but they will
eventually discover that they have courted a queen whose obsession
with revenge will ultimately transform their land into a realm of
the dead.

An indication of the level of callousness to which Kriemhild has
descended can be seen in her relationship to her son by Attila,
Ortlieb. While the latter may be a source of joy to Attila (1387.4)
and his people (1388.4), he is not depicted as being such to his
mother. Her chief concern is to have the child baptized (1388.1–
3), but this is a formality totally lacking in substance (or significance) for Kriemhild. She, herself, despite her explicit stated prej-
udice against Attila as a heathen (1248), never evinces more than
a superficial relationship to Christianity and God. In essence, she
is godless. Moreover, the absence of any maternal sentiment for
Ortlieb, reminiscent of her abandonment of young Gunther, is
symptomatic of her remarkable lack of responsibility toward the
future and the fate of those who may have to mold it. For Kriemhild,
the birth of Ortlieb has only a pragmatic function: it binds Attila,
together with his people, even closer to her. She either ignores, or

is no longer even aware of, its potential for much deeper significance as an act of renewal and rejuvenation.

We are witnessing the descent of Kriemhild into a realm of darkness, an unproductive world which contains no hope for the future but only the potential for mass destruction. Even the narrator has begun to associate her with the devil: "Ich waene der übel vâlant Kriemhilde daz geriet, / daz sie sich mit friuntschefte   von *Gunthere* schied" ("I believe it was the wicked devil who advised Kriemhild to break her pact of friendship with Gunther," 1394.1–2). It is important to note that while Kriemhild is still accorded the appellative "diu schoene" (1737.1), and, when the Burgundians arrive at Attila's court, may "approach the guests with all of the superficial gestures of courtliness,"[8] she is already possessed by "valschem muote" ("falsity, perfidy," 1737.2). Although the poet has previously depicted a Kriemhild capable of destructive deeds and words, he has hesitated to condemn her. Now, however, he, too, clearly aligns himself against her. This should not be taken as an indication that Siegfried's murder is being justified in the second half of the *Nibelungenlied,* but simply that Kriemhild's obsession with avenging her husband's death, regardless of the cost, is no longer regarded by anyone as warranted.

What can Kriemhild hope to achieve through a confrontation with Hagen? Siegfried is dead and cannot be brought back to life. The *hort,* however, is still intact, if concealed. By having Hagen divulge its location (something he is hardly prepared to do; see 1742.3–4), Kriemhild could restore at least the outer trappings of power associated with Siegfried, in a sense, regaining "a part" of her murdered husband, while at the same time publicly humiliating his murderer and her tormentor. But can Kriemhild really have expected Hagen to return the treasure? If she is simply recalling that an injustice was done to her in Worms and demonstrating that she has no intention of allowing Hagen and the others to forget it, she is playing into the hands of a master provocateur.

It is, in fact, Kriemhild who, once again, must contend with public humiliation at the hands of her adversary. His refusal to reveal the location of the *hort* (1742), an unabashed insult hurled at Kriemhild (1744.1), his refusal to part with his weapons (1745), along with Dietrich's reference to Kriemhild as a "vâlandinne" (1748.4), compromise the position of the queen of the Huns to an intolerable degree. Structurally, the scene has something in common with the departure scene in *Aventiure* 11; there, Kriemhild had been frustrated in her endeavor to acquire what was legally hers, and her husband, through his silence or rejection of her territories, had, in effect, sided with Hagen who had defied her. Once again, Kriemhild is not simply thwarted in her attempt to retrieve the *hort* and have Hagen respect her status. Dietrich, an ally, sides with the hero of Troneck and publicly insults the queen he purports to serve. We are witnessing here nothing less than a complete breakdown of courtly protocol. Dietrich's use of the word *vâlandinne* (1748.4) underscores his awareness of the extent to which Kriemhild has degenerated. Helmut de Boor has maintained that the use of this appellation so early by Dietrich tends to diminish its significance in the epic and is really a stylistic flaw on the part of the poet.[9] I would concur with Werner Hoffmann that the words spoken by Dietrich do, in fact, reflect the view of the author, that the hero's reproach is aimed at Kriemhild's "wicked and perfidious frame of mind, which has been twisted by hate,"[10] and that this is nothing less than diabolical. Kriemhild can no longer be regarded on the same plane as the others. She has aligned herself with demonic forces and, from Dietrich's perspective, has forfeited the respect normally accorded one of her position. Her isolation, both physical and spiritual, from the world in which she was raised, has allowed her to degenerate to this point. Kriemhild's quest for revenge at any cost has removed her spiritually from the mores of the court and the ideal of moderation. The poet does indeed appear to have lost sympathy with her,[11] undoubtedly because her obsession with revenge has caused her to ignore the inevitable consequences of her demand that Hagen be handed over to her.

It should be remembered that Kriemhild's plotting and her often open antagonism toward Hagen occur against the backdrop of a superficially harmonious atmosphere at Attila's court. Viewed from her perspective, she must contend with the presence of Siegfried's murderer while no one of stature, including her husband, appears willing to take up her case. She is concerned about establishing the legitimacy of her accusations against Hagen (note 1771), but the sole effect of this is merely to provoke her adversary even further (1781–83). Hagen even admits to having been responsible for Siegfried's death (1790–91), but this does not induce Dietrich or anyone else to call him to task for it. Failure on the part of any knight to act on her behalf ultimately forces Kriemhild herself into the role of military commander, although with little initial success (note 1848). Once Kriemhild has decided to launch an attack on the Burgundians with Hunnish troops, however, she both violates the rights of her guests and paves the way for Attila's involvement in the fray. That she should employ Ortlieb as a means of provoking Hagen (1912) is an indication of the extent to which she has abdicated her function as a mother figure, and of the fact that no maternal instinct will prevent her from utilizing the boy as a pawn. She may even have anticipated that Hagen's reaction will be violent and directed against Ortlieb when he learns of Bloedelin's massacre of the squires.

One point is clear: in the matter of Siegfried's murder, it is only Kriemhild who appears concerned about exacting revenge. No one else from any quarter or for any reason (excepting Bloedelin and his men) gives so much as a thought to calling Hagen to account. The twenty-six years which have passed since the death of the hero appear to have relativized the deed for everyone but Kriemhild; in her case, the sorrow has become all-encompassing. But the intensity of her vendetta against Hagen has escalated to the point that two entire peoples are now involved in a kind of tribal warfare. The conflict takes on dimensions which the queen herself may not have anticipated. Yet, immersed in her own grief and obsessed by hate and the desire for revenge, Kriemhild turns a blind eye to the suffering generated by her actions. By evolving into a narcissistic she-devil, she defies the *ordo* of society. Once hostilities have broken out on a grand scale and she has managed to secure safe conduct from the hall through the good offices of Dietrich, Kriemhild effectively outmaneuvers the hapless Attila for position of supreme commander. When the fighting finally subdues, the carnage occasioned by her unrelenting pursuit of revenge is evident: the warrior class of both the Burgundians and the Huns has, for all intents and purposes, been decimated.

There is no better testimony to the extent of Kriemhild's depravity than the reference to her joy once the fighting is over and Gunther and Hagen have been captured: "nâch ir vil starkem leide    dô wart si vroelîch genuoc" ("After the terrible misery she had suffered, she was now quite happy," 2353.4). The joy she now perceives is particularly perverse in the given situation. There is no thought for those who have been slaughtered, among them, her brothers Giselher and Gernot, as well as the noble Rüdeger. Hagen's final act of defiance, his adamant refusal to divulge the location of the *hort,* is expressed in terms intended to underscore the nonhuman nature of his opponent: "der sol dich, vâlandinne,    immer wol verholn sîn" ("It shall always remain hidden from you, you devil," 2371.4).

Even though she is the apparent "victor," Kriemhild remains "inferior" to Hagen, and fails to evoke anyone's sympathy. When she decapitates her defenseless adversary (after having had her brother Gunther slain), she violates a basic code of what is, essentially, a man's world. The act is unreservedly condemned even by her husband, Attila (2374), and when the hero of Troneck is avenged by Hildebrand, who hacks Kriemhild to pieces in full view of Attila, the Hunnish ruler does not utter the slightest hint of protest. Werner Hoffmann states simply: "She has been judged."[12] This is not the death of a human being, but rather the slaying of a monster.

## Siegfried

Siegfried, son of Siegmund and Sieglind of Xanten, was long considered by scholars of the *Nibelungenlied,* particularly those concerned with tracing its origins to myth, as the central figure of the epic. In according primacy to Kriemhild in this chapter, I have simultaneously implied that Siegfried, although a major figure in the work, does not hold the same fascination for the reader as his spouse. At the same time, however, it would not be imprudent to suggest that without Siegfried, Kriemhild would lose much of her complexity, and would hardly come to represent the ultimate danger to Worms and her own family.

Siegfried, like Kriemhild, is initially portrayed as a model of physical beauty (22.3), a prince who enjoys the unreserved respect of his contemporaries, a man who has already gained a widespread reputation for his strength and his exploits. In contrast to Kriemhild who, by the end of the first *Aventiure,* appears to have withdrawn from the public eye in order to spare herself potential grief, Siegfried stands at the center of courtly activity in Xanten. The second *Aventiure,* in which Siegfried is introduced, is laden with references to a vital, vibrant image of harmony, a world in which exemplary figures are presented as nonproblematical beings, and where the prospect of continued productivity seems to find concrete expression in Siegfried's knighting and his general and enthusiastic acceptance by the nobility of the land. In contrast to the poignant dichotomy

of the first *Aventiure,* where we are never allowed to forget that joy
and harmony are transitory conditions, and that death may be intimately linked to those who appear to personify much of that
superficial happiness, our introduction to Siegfried contains no allusions to future peril,[13] no ill portents in the form of disturbing
dreams, and above all, no realization on the part of the hero that
there is a darker side to life. Siegfried, as Hagen informs us in the
third *Aventiure,* has already had some remarkable experiences as a
young man. Events have transpired which, by their very nature and
consequence, set him apart from the rest of society, but the figure
remains dangerously unaware of the potential for catastrophe in the
courtly world. A certain naiveté characterizes Siegfried's behavior
throughout the first half of the *Nibelungenlied,* and this, complemented by his *übermuot* ("haughtiness," "arrogance") and his ig-
norance (or ignoring) of the deeper significance of words and actions,
constitutes one of the major factors responsible for bringing about
his death at the hands of Hagen. There is a basic difference between
Kriemhild and Siegfried with respect to the way in which each
perceives the world and his relationship to it. Kriemhild is conscious
of negative forces that are constantly present and which could prove
detrimental to her own person; rather than accept the good with
the bad as a basis for a balanced life, she seeks immunity from grief
as a recluse. Siegfried, by contrast, has no reason to doubt that the
success with which all his endeavors have hitherto been crowned,
will continue. He never suspects danger to his own person. And
yet, he embodies an incredible paradox, for he is certainly no stranger
to deceit, as his treatment of Brünhild demonstrates. Siegfried is,
in fact, a master deceiver in his own right, but he remains remarkably
unaware of the possibility that such deceit can also be directed
against himself, with devastating results.

Siegfried is not a man to be bothered by what might be considered
the everyday cares and worries of a medieval knight. His is a basically
carefree existence: "Den herren muoten selten    deheiniu herzen leit"
("No sorrow of any sort ever bothered the knight," 44.1). This
essentially nonchalant attitude characterizes Siegfried with terrible
consistency until his death. While it is directly responsible for some
of the fateful faux pas he commits, it is also the main reason that
the figure never runs the danger of evolving into a depraved creature
as happens with Kriemhild in the second part of the epic. Siegfried
is imprudent, arrogant, occasionally ruthless and callous, but he is

not given to the overt maliciousness and demonic scheming associated later with Kriemhild.

Removed from Worms, Siegfried presents no danger either to
himself or, it would appear, to anyone else. It is only when he is
associated with the "scoeniu meit" ("beautiful maiden," 44.2) of
Burgundy that the troubles to be faced by the prince are alluded
to: "von der er sît vil vreuden   und ouch arbeit gewan" ("He
would later know both happiness and great misfortune with her,"
44.4). His reaction to Siegmund's warning that the wooing of
Kriemhild cannot be undertaken without danger to his own person
underscores the difference between him and Kriemhild with regard
to the manner in which each responds to the threat of potential
grief. Whereas the Burgundian princess is quick to withdraw from
society in an effort to avoid such misfortune, Siegfried treats the
warning as a challenge, vowing to take by force that which the
Burgundians do not willingly hand over to him, including their
territories (55). His resolve to journey to Worms with no more than
eleven knights may, of course, be regarded as indicative of his innate
courage, but it is also testimony to his inclination toward reckless
behavior, and this, in turn, is rooted in his brash overconfidence.

Thus, even prior to his arrival in Worms, Siegfried is depicted
in an adversary relationship to the Burgundian court. Worms has
been identified as a place which holds not only the promise of a
future bride for Siegfried, but also the prospect of a clash with forces
antagonistic toward him. Yet it acts like a magnet upon Siegfried,
for if he was originally attracted to Worms solely by Kriemhild's
presence there, Siegmund's forewarning of the dangers which his
son may encounter elicits an immediate assertion by Siegfried that
he will, if necessary, bring the Burgundians to their knees.

Arrival episodes in the *Nibelungenlied* can be of profound significance in establishing the subsequent relationship between "guest"
and "host." What is said and done by the leading personalities in
such instances may determine the course of events for entire peoples
as well as for the individuals immediately involved. A permanent
bond or a cleft may be formed between those receiving and those
being received. This is particularly true of the first meeting between
Siegfried and the Burgundians, an encounter not destined to win
for Siegfried the unqualified respect and trust of his hosts. His
explanation of why he has come does not betray the slightest hint
of affection for Kriemhild; in fact, she is not mentioned at all. The

reader wonders whether Siegfried's initial intent to woo the princess has become totally sublimated into a resolve to deprive the Burgundians of their territory: "ich wil an iu ertwingen,     swaz ir muget hân: / lant unde bürge,     daz sol mir werden undertân" ("I shall divest you by force of whatever you might own. Both your lands and your castles shall be mine," 110.3–4). Siegfried's determination to take territory from the Burgundians is indicative of his tendency to act, if not blindly, then certainly without reasonable restraint and reflection when it is a question of enhancing his reputation. [14] The matter of a potential union between himself and Kriemhild has given way entirely to what must be considered by the Burgundians as his unwarranted demands, his "will to power." Siegfried's behavior at this point—let us not forget that he is addressing the king of a powerful nation—represents a radical departure from the moderation advocated and expected by the courtly period in which the work was written. Siegfried has, in effect, challenged the very status quo of Worms, an act which, regardless of the outcome, must establish him in the minds of some as a potential eradicator of that order. A more perceptive Burgundian, such as Hagen, will already have recognized in Siegfried some of the elements which led Gottfried Weber to designate him as "a super-dimensional . . . quite uncontrolled *Naturkraft*." [15]

Siegfried provokes on two levels: first, through his unabashed claim to their territory, he calls into question Burgundian sovereignty; second, having noted how his father singled out Hagen as the one to be particularly wary of (54.1–3), Siegfried appears intent on calling him out: "müet iuch daz, her Hagene,     daz ich gesprochen hân, / sô sol ich lâzen kiesen,     daz die hende mîn / wellent vil gewaltec     hie zen Burgonden sîn" ("If what I have said displeases you, lord Hagen, then I shall make it quite clear that I intend to be the one giving orders here in Burgundy," 122.2–4). But it is not the only time that Hagen must endure a taunt from a feisty Siegfried. In strophe 125, the latter all but challenges him directly: "War umbe bîtet Hagene     und ouch Ortwîn, / daz er niht gâhet strîten     mit den friwenden sîn, / der er hie sô manegen     zen Burgonden hât?" ("Why do Hagen and Ortwin tarry and, together with Hagen's many friends here in Burgundy, not take up the fight?" 125.1–3). This is not the type of snub which a man of Hagen's stature is likely to forgive, or forget.

One might well inquire as to why hostilities do not break out on the spot. Were Siegfried to pursue his claims without relenting, it is difficult to imagine that the Burgundians, despite their knowledge of his virtual invulnerability, would be left with any alternative but to meet force with force. That such a situation does not arise is due solely to the fact that Siegfried, whose thoughts have returned to Kriemhild, allows himself to be mollified by the (sincere) gestures of hospitality and the offer of land made by Gunther. The time may never again arise when Siegfried would even consider making such demands on the Burgundians, but there are clearly aspects of his nature which are totally alien to the courtly setting. Hagen, in particular, is well informed about Siegfried's youth, his journey to the Other World with its giants and dwarfs, his acquisition of the immense treasure of the Nibelungs, as well as his fight with the dragon whose blood has made him almost invulnerable. Siegfried has been exposed to a world far removed from that of the court. Moreover, he has returned from that world after having been noticeably affected by it. Siegfried's initiation into knighthood (described at length in the second *Aventiure*) has been preceded by his self-initiation into the realm of the Other World. He is no longer on the same level of awareness or physical prowess as other knights within courtly society, and it is little wonder that he is never depicted as one who enjoys a close relationship with any other knight. (In contrast, we note the bond of friendship between Hagen and Volker in the second half of the *Nibelungenlied*.) While he may be aware of another level of existence, however, Siegfried is dangerously insensitive to the *modus operandi* of the world to which he returns, and his failure to comprehend fully the significance of his words and actions (many of which are characterized by his overt arrogance) plays a major role in bringing about his own downfall.

In those instances in which Siegfried provides assistance to the Burgundians, namely, in the war against the Saxons and Danes (fourth *Aventiure*), and in the wooing and subsequent taming of Brünhild for Gunther (*Aventiuren* six through ten), there can be no question that his prime motivation is to acquire Kriemhild as his bride: "Jane lob' ichz niht sô verre    durch die liebe dîn / sô durch dîne swester,    daz scoene magedîn" ("It is not to acquire your love that I will promise to help, but rather I do it for the sake of your beautiful sister," 388. 1–2). Siegfried has intimated to Gunther at an earlier point that he wishes to be considered one of his friends

(see strophe 156), but this does not deter him from making un-
necessary and insensitive remarks such as the one above. He also
does not realize that the assistance which he provides to the Burgundians cannot help but make the latter increasingly more dependent on him. Nowhere is this more apparent than in the series of
events surrounding the wooing of Brünhild.

Whether in his initial demands for Burgundian territory or in
his subsequent handling of the Saxon/Danish question, Siegfried's
self-confidence and his faith in the validity of his aims are never in
doubt. The same cannot be said for his participation in the Brünhild
mission. It is the one (ultimately fatal) instance in which he acts
against his better judgment. His involvement entangles him in a
web of deceit largely of his own making which eventually costs him
his life.

Siegfried's first reaction to Gunther's assertion that he will risk
his life to make Brünhild his queen is unmistakable: "Daz wil ich
widerrâten" ("I'd advise against it," 330.1). He is, after all, aware
of the "vreislîche sit" ("horrible ways," 330.2; see also 340.2) of
the queen of Iceland. More important, however, is the fact that
Siegfried appears to have had some prior liaison with Brünhild.[16]
Not only does he know the way to her kingdom (378), about her
harsh manners with suitors (330), and the attire to be worn in
Iceland (344), it is he who is first greeted by Brünhild. She assumes
that it is Siegfried who wishes to woo her (416.2–3). The intimation
seems clear: while parsimonious with respect to details, the poet
has dropped "clues" which would indicate that Siegfried and Brünhild are anything but strangers to one another. The three tests
established by the queen (javelin throw, hurling the boulder, leaping
over the boulder) are designed less to eliminate potential suitors
than to determine who is, in fact, the perfect match for her. Siegfried
has no allusions about the outcome were Gunther to be left to his
own devices. But by deceiving Brünhild, he deceives himself, for
he defies the *ordo* of that Other World into which he had been
initiated as a youth. Does not Siegfried defy fate? Was he not
originally destined to wed Brünhild?

The events which transpire after the wooing party has landed in
Iceland provide a graphic demonstration of one of the main structural
threads of the epic, the dichotomy between *Sein* and *Schein,* between
reality and appearance. In this instance, the dichotomy is known
to Siegfried and the Burgundians who accompany him, as well as

to the reader. From Brünhild's perspective, however, that which she observes and subsequently hears corresponds to reality, as much as she may privately wonder how a figure such as Siegfried could be subordinate to anyone. The forms in which the deceit concocted by Siegfried is manifested can be defined as follows: (1) metaphysical, (2) visual, (3) oral, and (4) physical. The very thought of enabling Gunther to marry Brünhild is tantamount to gross deception; this is intensified by Siegfried's "act of subservience" in holding the bridle of Gunther's horse upon arriving in Iceland (397), and by his assertion that Gunther is his lord (420.4). When Siegfried, made invisible by the *Tarnkappe* ("magic hood") obtained from Albrich, defeats Brünhild in the threefold ordeal, he confirms that only he could ever be considered a suitable partner for the queen. This deception attains its pinnacle when, in the tenth *Aventiure,* Siegfried assumes Gunther's place in the bedroom and "tames" Brünhild in a vicious wrestling match, robbing her of her superhuman strength.

Why does Siegfried turn his back on Brünhild and ignore the significance of his actions? Despite the various characteristics they have in common, the hero of Xanten is clearly not attracted to the queen of Iceland. The answer seems simple: for the sake of Kriemhild. And yet, one may further query as to why his love for her, a woman whom he scarcely knows, is so all-encompassing, powerful enough to make him blind to the fact that his "rightful" partner is Brünhild. Certainly Kriemhild's widely acclaimed beauty has much to do with Siegfried's infatuation, and it may not be exaggerated to consider it to be of a demonic nature.[17] There may also be another reason underlying Siegfried's callous treatment of Brünhild. By defeating her in the ordeals in Iceland, he makes it possible for Gunther to bring her to Worms, that is, he effects her physical removal from the Other World sphere. His "taming" of her on the nuptial bed is not only a "service" to Gunther. It is simultaneously a confirmation of his view that a woman's place in courtly society is subordinate to that of her husband. He is "upholding the honor" of men (see, in particular, strophe 673), while at the same time forcing Brünhild to conform to courtly mores. It is quite possible that Siegfried considers Brünhild to be a threat to society in her "Amazon-like" state.

In essence, Siegfried does appear to conform, or, at least, want to conform, to courtly society. His own brashness and immoderate behavior in the third *Aventiure* were tempered by his thoughts of

Kriemhild who, at that point, would have seemed the personification of the cultivated nobility. That he does not fully succeed in reintegrating himself into that courtly world is evinced by his retention of the *Tarnkappe* and his return to the land of the Nibelungs in the eighth *Aventiure*. Without realizing its ramifications, Siegfried is caught in a dilemma, trapped, in a sense, between two very different worlds, a figure attempting desperately to adapt to courtly society yet unable (or unwilling) to turn his back on the Other World into which he was initiated as a youth.

Why does Siegfried die? It is a question that continues to be addressed by scholars of the *Nibelungenlied*, [18] and with good reason. Are we to accept the most obvious explanation—the dishonoring of the Burgundian court through Kriemhild's tactlessness in the minster scene—as the prime factor behind the murder? Or are there other, deeper reasons? The text offers considerable evidence to support the theory that the motives for Siegfried's death are indeed multifaceted. They are to be found in his relationship to Hagen, in particular, and to the Burgundians in general. At the same time, we should not exclude the possibility that his death has a "cosmic" significance. Siegfried's provocation of individual and clan alike upon his arrival in Worms has been alluded to above. From the outset a state of tension has existed between them, the Burgundians being cast into Siegfried's shadow (although this is attributable, in large part, to their own lack of character), subject to any of the superman's whims, with only Kriemhild as a trump card. The dependency increases as a result of the Saxon-Danish war, before which Siegfried had suggested (albeit naively) that Gunther remain at home and tend to the women (174), and in the course of which Hagen must abdicate primacy as military leader to the newcomer. The acquisition of Brünhild for Gunther both accentuates this dependency and makes Siegfried party to a secret whose revelation can only cause Worms great dishonor. Siegfried's marriage to Kriemhild proves detrimental to Worms in that it does not create a strong alliance, but rather two rival power centers once Kriemhild begins to assert her position. It also leads to the divulging of the secret. But it has been Siegfried's denial of a "natural right and obligation," a partnership with Brünhild, which has brought about such a crisis. In no way can Siegfried be absolved of blame for the consequences.

Siegfried's overbearing self-confidence, his apparent belief that he can master any situation, lead him into a false sense of security which he couples with incredible naiveté. Although he is sincere in his offer of friendship to Gunther (156), and undoubtedly believes that he has always demonstrated fidelity toward the Burgundians (989.3), Siegfried consistently evinces a lack of sensitivity toward others and an incapacity to comprehend the deeper significance of his actions. We note that, despite his emphasis on friendship, he himself remains without any real friends up to his death. His spontaneous, often overbearing manner, his way of "looking at the world," are basically narcissistic, characteristic of a "loner." Siegfried represents a danger to society, not just to one or several members of the Burgundian court. This is largely due to his unpredictability, however, and not to malice aforethought; and this distinguishes him from Kriemhild. As it turns out, however, Siegfried dead represents a greater threat to Worms than Siegfried alive, and Hagen's reassurances to the Burgundian kings that all their worries are over ("ez hât nu allez ende     unser sorge unt unser leit," 993.2) constitute, perhaps, the most ironic miscalculation in the epic.

## Hagen

Few figures in medieval German literature are as complex as Hagen, as ambiguous in their motivations, and as obscure in their origins. He is a man of many hats: chief counselor to Gunther and, at least before Siegfried's arrival (and once again after his death), principal military leader among the Burgundians, a person endowed with considerable knowledge of matters pertaining to life beyond the court at Worms, a "soothsayer" of sorts, whose contacts to Other World figures such as the water sprites in the twenty-fifth *Aventiure* contribute to his image as a "dark figure," whom some have referred to as "demonic."[19] Hagen is a man who cherishes power, above all for the Burgundian court. He is an individual who has few scruples when it is a question of enhancing the court's prestige. His loyalty toward the Burgundians has been considered exemplary, and his heroic stance at the conclusion of the epic the epitome of the "heroic spirit." However, Hagen is a man endowed with a considerable amount of "übermuot," a figure whose "untriuwe" ("infidelity") toward Siegfried is roundly condemned by the poet (note 981.4), a counselor whose advice proves catastrophic for the family with which he clearly identifies, a warrior whose limitations become all too clear in his fight against Gelphrat in Bavaria (note 1613).

Hagen is depicted in two major roles: as the adversary and eventual murderer of Siegfried, and as the adversary and eventual "victim" of Kriemhild. In the first case, the portrayal is decidedly negative, in the second, the sympathy of the author, the other characters in the work, and the reader, seems clearly aligned with him. As we have already witnessed, from the outset, the relationship between Hagen and Siegfried is characterized by tension, not overt, concrete antagonism, but rather a subdued animosity on Hagen's side which ferments below the surface of visible actions until it is accorded ultimate expression in his attack on Siegfried.

While it is admittedly difficult to contemplate the possibility of a close relationship between Hagen and Siegfried under any circumstances, there is abundant textual evidence to support the thesis that Hagen is more than willing to arrive at some sort of modus vivendi with the superman. His reasons are openly pragmatic: better to have Siegfried as a "friend" and ally than as an enemy. But the unjustified taunts of the hero from Xanten (122.2–4; 125.1–3) will have left their mark. His honor as an individual, as well as the collective honor of the Burgundian ruling class, has been compromised by the unwarranted demands and blatant arrogance of Siegfried. If this honor is further tarnished by a growing dependence on the latter, one might well expect Hagen to undertake any measure necessary to put some distance between Siegfried and Worms. Nevertheless, he is the one responsible for having Siegfried commit himself to the war against the Saxons and the Danes, and it is his counsel—in direct contrast to that offered by Siegfried—which Gunther heeds in his quest to make Brünhild his queen. In both instances, Hagen allows the possibility of enhancing the reputation of Worms to win out over good sense. In the second case, the advice is deadly. If we subscribe to the notion that Hagen takes a special delight in manipulating Siegfried, then we must also note that it is ironic how his suggestions set events in motion which ultimately help to bring about the demise of the Burgundian Empire. Even when he encounters Brünhild in Iceland and, realizing that Gunther is quite out of his league, refers to the queen as "des tiuveles wîp" ("the devil's woman," 438.4; see also 450.4), Hagen does not retreat.

Siegfried's *superbia* (note 680.1) may well have played a significant role in his death, but it should not be assumed that Hagen was acting totally out of altruism when he killed him. The excuse offered in strophe 867, that Siegfried should die because he has boasted

about having bedded Brünhild—something which Siegfried is prepared to deny under oath—could certainly be considered a valid
enough reason for dealing with him. The harm done the court is
real enough. But it is only one in a series of "incidents" that have
allowed Hagen's animosity toward Siegfried to become intensified.
It is difficult to believe that he does not mount a personal vendetta
against Siegfried. Moreover, with Siegfried dead, there is a distinct
possibility that the Burgundians may acquire his *hort,* a veritably
unlimited source of power to which Hagen has already had occasion
to refer: "hort der Nibelunge    beslozzen hât sîn hant. / hey sold
er komen immer    in der Burgonden lant!" ("He managed to win
the treasure of the Nibelungs. If only one day it might be brought
to Burgundy!" 774.3–4).

It is not unlikely that all these factors play a role in Hagen's
decision to kill Siegfried. His reference, after the murder, to the
dissipation of the Burgundians' "sorge" and "leit" ("worries and
cares," 993.2) is ambiguous. What is not, however, is the poet's
condemnation of the act, underscored by at least ten references to
the treachery ("untriuwe, meinraete") occurring from the latter part
of the fourteenth *Aventiure* through the sixteenth (876.2; 881.1;
887.3; 906.3; 911.4; 915.4; 916.2; 971.4; 981.4; 988.4).

Had Hagen been content simply to murder Siegfried, a later
reconciliation between Hagen and Kriemhild might have been effected. What is quite apparent, however, is that he is just as eager
to hurt Kriemhild. From his perspective, this may seem justified.
Since becoming Siegfried's wife, Kriemhild has demonstrated a
marked tendency to ignore the interests of Worms. She has, in fact,
done a serious injury to the court in her public confrontation and
altercation with Brünhild before the minster. When Hagen decides
to lay Siegfried's corpse before Kriemhild's chamber, he is motivated
by "grôzer übermüete" and "eislîcher râche" ("great arrogance" and
"icy revenge," 1003.1–2). It is deliberate provocation on his part,
perhaps an indication of his belief that any embarrassment caused
the Burgundian court cannot be avenged too severely.

While both the poet and the reader may be inclined, at this point,
to condemn Hagen, it should be observed that he is the only Burgundian who acts with consistency, even if this implies complete
ruthlessness. When he deprives Kriemhild of the *hort* and sinks it
in the Rhine, he clearly has the interests of Worms (as well as his
own) in mind. What is remarkable about Hagen is his awareness

that Kriemhild could still become a tremendous liability to Worms. He alone recognizes the potential danger in her union with Attila: "habt ir rehte sinne, sô wirt ez wol behuot, / ob sis joch volgen wolde, daz irz nimmer getuot" ("If you haven't taken leave of your senses, you'll prevent her from ever going through with this, even if she wants to," 1203.3–4). One senses that Hagen knows that as long as Kriemhild remains in Worms, her ability to do the Burgundians harm is greatly reduced; removed from Worms, however, she may be considered less a sister of Gunther and his brothers than an enemy of the court. Her union with Siegfried has already demonstrated how formidable an adversary she can be.

The reader is struck by the manner in which the poet rivets his attention throughout the second half of the *Nibelungenlied* on Kriemhild's obsession with revenge and her inexhaustible capacity for lamenting the death of Siegfried. At the same time, he no longer has an unkind word for Hagen, but rather seems intent upon replacing the image of the disloyal murderer with that of the loyal retainer prepared to serve his king to the death. Why this shift in emphasis? Is Siegfried's murder not just as deplorable thirteen years after the fact as it was on the day it was committed? The answer offered implicitly by the poet seems to be a categorical "No!" Siegfried was quite incorrect when he assumed that his murderers would be held in contempt by decent knights (990.4). Neither Hagen's reputation, nor that of the Burgundian royal family, seem to have suffered the slightest injury. In view of the hospitality extended them, particularly Hagen, by both Rüdeger and Dietrich, the impression could easily be gained that "decent knights" not only accepted Siegfried's death, perhaps as being quite legal,[20] but that as a result they also accorded Hagen even greater stature as a warrior. There is, after all, no outcry, no calling for a reckoning at any time after the murder from anyone other than Kriemhild. Even Siegmund, Siegfried's father, never pursues the matter once he returns to Xanten.

The poet does not appear at all concerned with any "legal" resolution of the problem. We have witnessed how he has laid the foundation for an unrelenting dichotomy between Kriemhild and Hagen in the first part of the *Nibelungenlied;* and all of his skill is employed in the second half to intensify the conflict. It has begun to take on entirely new dimensions, however. Left in Worms, the most Kriemhild might have achieved was a "knife in the back," had Hagen ever let down his guard. Removed to Hungary as Attila's queen, her "private" feud with Hagen escalates, of necessity, to the level of intertribal warfare. Her obsession with revenge may be described as demonic, but Hagen's darker side is also consistently in evidence, despite his basically sympathetic portrayal in the second half of the epic.

With Kriemhild's invitation to her brothers to journey to Hungary, Hagen realizes that nothing has changed, and that a very real danger awaits them were Gunther to accept. Of one thing he is now convinced: Kriemhild's anger is not directed solely at him. The Burgundian kings, despite the earlier reconciliation with their sister, will lose both "êre" and "lîp" (1461.3), if they accept the invitation. Ultimately, Hagen is fully aware of the fact that he is the one Kriemhild really wants, but that she will not spare her brothers in order to get at him. One might well ask why he does not sacrifice himself, journey to Hungary ahead of the Burgundians and face Kriemhild alone. The fact that he does not may be an indication of his keen perception of the significance of *êre* within society. A lonely death suffered by him at Attila's court will not enhance the honor of the Burgundian clan. But the answer may also lie in the abstract concept of fate to which Hagen subscribes: for better or for worse, he is inextricably linked to the Burgundian royal house.

Compared with Siegfried, Hagen is the greater hero. Siegfried embodies all of the outward trappings of the hero figure, but we are granted very little insight into the workings of his mind. For him, spontaneity is paramount. Hagen is more inclined to reflect before acting. Siegfried dies with no awareness of what is to befall him. His naiveté prevents him from recognizing the "darker" workings of the world. Hagen's awareness of such ominous forces places him in the position of knowing his destiny. The prediction of the water sprite that *all* who journey to Hungary will die there (1540)—duplicating the message imparted in Ute's dream that *all* the birds of the realm had died (1509)—confirms what Hagen has already known to be his own fate as well as that of the kings. It catches him off guard, however, because now, for the first time, he is confronted with the full extent of the disaster to follow. This encounter is esoteric, the only truly supernatural event in the second half of the *Nibelungenlied*. Its exclusively mythical nature serves to underscore Hagen's uniqueness. We realize that he and Siegfried have more in common than might appear on the surface. Hagen's ties to the nonhuman world mark him as a being set apart from the king whom he serves. They can be explained, of course, by the *Nibelungen* tradition,[21] but here they seem to effect a mental elevation in Hagen, to raise him to the level of a "ritual" figure who "knows" something which will affect the destiny of thousands of others. Hagen has, in a sense, undergone a kind of initiation; when he returns to the Burgundians after his encounter with the water sprites, he is endowed with a greater sense of awareness of the world and his role in it, as well as the course of events in the future. He senses an obligation to assume the role of "spiritual" as well as physical "Protector" *(trôst)* of the Burgundians. It is Hagen's inner comportment here and elsewhere, in the face of inexorable fate, which constitutes his heroism.

From the departure of the Burgundians for Hungary until the conclusion of the epic, Hagen is depicted as the de facto leader of the group. It is he who secures a way across the Danube by killing a ferryman (1562) and assuming his role in order to transport thousands (!) of Burgundian knights and their squires to the other bank. As such, he conjures up the image of a Germanic Charon figure, and his destruction of the vessel once they are all on the other side (1581.3) lends finality to the crossing over from the one world to the next. From the twenty-fifth *Aventiure* on, he is, in fact, the leader of a party already marked for death, although the Burgundians, despite the fact that they have been told by Hagen of what lies in store for them (1587–90), do not convey the impression that they are constantly aware of just how serious the situation is. While they may tend to accept the superficial merriment and festivity prevailing in Rüdeger's Bechelaren, and later in the Hunnish court, as a reflection of the actual state of affairs, Hagen remains consistently cognizant of the blatant dichotomy between *Sein* and *Schein*. But his ability to distinguish between these two poles in no way anticipates a possible reconciliation between himself and Kriemhild. He is fully aware that the latter's quest for revenge cannot be tempered. He and the others will die; the only thing that matters is that they die with honor.

Few scenes of mutual antagonism and provocation in literature are more vividly painted than those involving Hagen and Kriemhild following the arrival of the Burgundians in Hungary. These are dramatic highlights of the poem, for it is during their encounters that the dichotomy between appearance and reality begins to dis-

sipate. Hagen's tightening of his helmet in Kriemhild's presence
(1737.4) is provocative, and this is soon augmented by bitter sarcasm. In response to Kriemhild's query as to what the Burgundians
might have brought her from Worms, Hagen claims that he has
not brought her a damned thing ("Jâ bringe ich iu den tiuvel,"
1744.1). It does not take blatant defiance on Hagen's part (such as
in 1744.4, when he refuses to give up his, that is, Siegfried's,
sword) for Kriemhild to be grieved. The very sight of the warrior
suffices to make her weep (1762–63; note also 1781–83, when
Hagen refuses to rise in her presence). Hagen does not have anything
to lose, of course. He is convinced that his death is not far off, and
seems intent upon retaliating against Kriemhild in his own way for
her manipulations.

Unlike Siegfried, Hagen is capable of forming genuine friendships
with other knights. The most obvious example is Volker, but there
can be no doubt that Hagen also enjoys the respect of Rüdeger,
Dietrich, and, even after the conclusion of hostilities, Attila. All
are aware, of course, that Hagen was the man directly responsible
for Siegfried's death, but this appears to be of no consequence to
them when it comes to their judgment of the figure.

Just prior to the outbreak of war between the Burgundians and
Huns, an opportunity arises whereby, one might argue, it would
be possible to ward off catastrophe. Sighting the Burgundians fully
armed on their way to the minster, Attila immediately suspects that
someone has wronged them (1861–62). At this point, is it not
possible for Hagen and his companions to speak up and inform their
host of Kriemhild's plot against them, and of the provocations that
have already taken place? Why does Hagen tell Attila a lie, that it
is a Burgundian custom to go armed for three days at a festival
(1863.2–3)? It would appear that this is nothing less than a challenge hurled at Kriemhild, a sign that the Burgundians are prepared
to fight, despite the hopelessness of their situation. Kriemhild, by
implication, understands full well the damage which might be done
Hagen's honor by his divulging the truth of the matter to her
husband. While she may recognize Hagen's inner strength and
stature, she despises him for it: "wie rehte fîentliche    si im under
diu ougen sach!" ("How savage was the glance she cast him!" 1864.2).
Ever aware of the basic dichotomy between his major protagonists,
the poet attributes the Burgundians' silence to their haughtiness
("vil starken übermuot," 1865.4), which may well reflect a less

than veiled criticism of a code of honor and behavior that leaves no room for compromise, preferring even mass slaughter and devastation to the possibility of appearing cowardly before one's peers.

If guilt is to be apportioned among the major figures for the apocalyptic conclusion of the *Nibelungenlied,* Hagen, despite his decidedly "positive" portrayal (in comparison with his depiction in the first half of the epic), must be accorded his share. Yet the poet, unlike his inferior "successor," the anonymous author of the *Klage,* does not approach the catastrophe he paints from this perspective at all. He is solely concerned with the unravelling and drastic resolution of the antipathy between Kriemhild and Hagen, not with ascertaining or assigning culpability. Moreover, unlike the question of motivation for Siegfried's death, one that could be regarded as multidimensional, the feud in which Kriemhild and Hagen are engaged is characterized by clear motivation from beginning to end.

Hagen's decapitation of Ortlieb, whose sole function appears to have been to provide an extension of Kriemhild's provocative wiles, does not give the poet cause to alter in any manner the stature he has hitherto accorded the figure: "Dô sluoc daz kint Ortlieben Hagen der helt guot" ("Then Hagen, that fine hero, slew the child Ortlieb," 1961.1). There is no sarcasm or irony implied in the use of the epithet "guot," and, even as a formulaic device, it is hardly probable that it would be used in such a context without the realization on the part of the poet of the stark contrast it affords to the preceding act. There is no hint of condemnation from anyone except, of course, Attila, who now has no choice but to enter the dispute.

Hagen's killing of Ortlieb, a radical response to all of Kriemhild's machinations, simultaneously reflects his own conviction that there is no hope left for a better future, which the young prince certainly symbolized to the Huns. For Hagen as well as Kriemhild, only the present matters. They have, in essence, chosen to ignore the potential and real consequences of their actions or, at least, have elected to accept whatever may come about in their wake. By subordinating everything else to the resolution of their mutual animosities, they have abandoned any pretense of adhering to courtly mores, particularly the virtue of moderation.

Throughout the *Nibelungenlied* one witnesses a certain distance between Hagen and the Burgundian kings. Their relationship is, at times, strained, although there can be little doubt that Hagen

regards his service to the royal family as his ultimate calling in life.
But until the thirty-fourth *Aventiure,* in the midst of the conflict
against the Huns, it is impossible to discern a close, human bond
between Hagen and his liege lords. When, however, Giselher suggests that the bodies of (seven thousand!) Huns who have fallen in
battle be removed from the palace and declares that he is firmly
resolved to sell his life dearly (2010–12), Hagen's response is immediate and enthusiastic:

> "Sô wol mich sölhes herren,"     sprach dô Hagene.
> "der rât enzaeme niemen        wan einem degene,
> den uns mîn junger herre     hiute hât getân.
> des muget ir Burgonden       alle vroelîche stân." (2012)

(Hagen said: "I am fortunate to have such a lord. What Giselher has just
said are words that could only be spoken by a true warrior. Now you
Burgundians may certainly take heart.")

At no time previous in the text have we encountered such an overt
demonstration of respect on Hagen's part for any member of the
Burgundian royal family. Yet, Mowatt and Sacker offer a somewhat
cynical commentary on Hagen's reaction to Giselher's resolve: "Hagen
may well be pleased: at last the kings are seeing things his way;
that is, they have ceased to be kings and have become fighting-
men."[22] This may be quite unfair. One could maintain that, from
Hagen's perspective, the kings have begun to act as one would
expect of kings, not, of course, in accordance with the tenets of a
more genteel, and idealized, courtly society, but rather as Germanic
warrior kings at the head of a *comitatus.* Mowatt and Sacker regard
this transition as a "dragging down"[23] of the kings to Hagen's level,
that is, to a level at which only heroes count. This very process of
transition could, however, be just as easily, and—considering a
medieval rather than a modern framework of values—more justifiably, interpreted as an elevation of the kings from the static and
sterile existence they have hitherto maintained to the position of
true heroes displaying an exemplary attitude in the face of death.
    If Hagen's killing of Siegfried at the stream in the sixteenth
*Aventiure* is the low point of his existence,[24] his leadership of the
Burgundians in the Great Hall of Attila, coupled with his defiance
of Kriemhild in the final scenes of the epic, is certainly the high-

point. He is here in his element, the "trôst" of the Nibelungs (compare 1526.2; 1726.4), and when the hall is set on fire and the Burgundians begin to thirst, Hagen urges them to drink the blood of the dead about them: "ir edeln ritter guot, / swen twinge durstes nôt,    der trinke hie daz bluot. / daz ist in solher hitze    noch bezzer danne wîn" ("You noble knights, whoever of you is plagued by thirst should drink this blood. In such heat it is even better than wine," 2114.1b–3). Apart from the fact that the advice is well given under the circumstances and does, in fact, fulfill a practical function, the scene does present Hagen as a demonic figure. There is no reason to speculate on the possibility of "Christian symbolism"[25] with regard to the drinking of the blood. Neither God nor Christianity play any role in the *Nibelungenlied* at this point, and the argument that it is precisely for this reason that the Burgundians are destined to die to a man lacks any substantiating textual evidence. To be sure, there is a formal allusion to "God's mercy" in 2112.3, and no one would seriously contend that the Burgundians are not "Christians" in the formal sense of the word. Hagen had encouraged them to attend a last mass, and has referred to "got dem rîchen" ("Almighty God," 1855.3). But his Christianity, like that of the others, is formal, hence superficial, without any real substance or, for that matter, consistency. The poet devotes three full strophes to the blood-drinking episode, depicting graphically how the Burgundians are imbued with new strength by drinking directly from the wounds of the slain warriors (2115–17). This is less reminiscent of the Eucharist than of the superstitious belief in the healing and rejuvenating power of blood. (Compare also Hartmann von Aue's *Der arme Heinrich* in this regard.)

The physical stamina and prowess in battle demonstrated by Hagen are complemented by his inner superiority when compared to Kriemhild in their final confrontation. The poet regards him as the "küenesten recken    der ie swert getruoc" ("the bravest knight who ever bore arms," 2353.3). He and Gunther are the only members of the Burgundian party who survive the various attacks on the Great Hall. It is clear to Hagen that the prophecies of the water sprite (as well as the dream-vision of Ute) are to be fulfilled. In this moment of military defeat, he has but one way left to spite Kriemhild: to refuse to divulge the location of Siegfried's *hort*. This involves him in a particularly problematical act. By telling Kriemhild that he has sworn to keep the hiding place secret as long as his lords

live (2368), he is effectively sending Gunther to his doom. The
reader cannot help but consider the possibility that Hagen fears his
king may once again waver, perhaps even effect a reconciliation
between himself and Kriemhild and provide her with the location
of the treasure. There is no textual evidence to substantiate Hagen's
claim that he had ever made such a "pact" with the Burgundian
rulers, and we must, therefore, conclude that what he tells Kriemhild is calculated to send Gunther to his death. This may be attributed, however, to Hagen's perception of an ethic which transcends
life itself. For Gunther to continue living after having divulged
where the treasure lies hidden would seriously compromise both his
own and the family's honor. Hagen cannot discount the possibility
that this could occur; in a paradoxical way, he, the "Protector" of
the Burgundians, assures that their honor is upheld by manipulating
Kriemhild into a position in which she commits fratricide. His own
fate is unalterable; he does not doubt for a moment that he will
die, regardless of what he might tell Kriemhild. Though physically
defeated, Hagen shows himself to be inwardly superior to Kriemhild, and manipulates the queen in accordance with his code of
honor. His final words are testimony to his heroic comportment
and are symbolic of his inner victory over Kriemhild:

> "Nu ist von Burgonden     der edel künec tôt,
> Gîselher der junge     unde ouch her Gêrnôt.
> den schaz den weiz nu niemen     wan got unde mîn:
> der sol dich, vâlandinne,     immer wol verholn sîn." (2371)

("Now the noble King of Burgundy is dead, as well as young Giselher
and Lord Gernot. Only God and I know where the treasure is hidden,
and it will always remain hidden from you, you devil!")

If hubris is an integral part of Hagen the hero, the demonic,
dark figure,[26] it appears to be a characteristic which is not unreservedly condemned by the poet. Hagen's individualism, which, to
quite a degree, determines the fateful course taken by the Burgundians, is rather an object of considerable admiration. In Hagen the
poet incorporates diverse antithetical elements, so that a final "judgment" of the figure must avoid a stereotype. In Hagen we find
wisdom and restraint, but also ambition, the will to power, as well
as a consistent association with the darker side of life. Perhaps Hagen

understood how dangerous Siegfried could be to the courtly world, because he, Hagen, had himself intimate knowledge of the Other World and its potential for unleashing chaos among mankind. Hagen embodies both the demonic and the purely heroic in a type of majestic sublimity which the reader, like the poet, cannot help but admire, although, as Gottfried Weber has stated, not without a shudder.[27]

## Brünhild

Neither Brünhild nor Siegfried appears in the second half of the *Nibelungenlied,* although it has become abundantly clear that the hero of Xanten is constantly in the mind of his widow. It is also possible that Kriemhild identified the *hort* with her late husband, and that regaining it would have been, in at least a symbolic sense, regaining a part of Siegfried. Siegfried remains a major figure even after his demise through the obsessive manner in which Kriemhild remembers and vows to avenge him. There is virtually no trace of Brünhild, however. Is it warranted, then, to include her among the major figures? The most compelling reason for doing so is the role she plays in contributing to Siegfried's demise and helping to set in motion those events which lead to the destruction of the Burgundians and Huns. Moreover, her fate is inextricably linked to that of Siegfried; it is also difficult to imagine that the latter would have come to such an untimely end had he refrained from deceiving Brünhild and removing her from Iceland to the court at Worms.

While Brünhild may, along with Kriemhild, be accorded the formulaic epithet "unmâzen scoene"[28] ("incredibly beautiful," 326.3), she is also designated by Gunther as a "vreislîchez wîp" ("a terrible woman," 655.4). How perceptively the poet remarks: "ir gelîche enheine    man wesse ninder mê" ("No one will ever know her equal," 326.2). Isolated from the courtly world in her castle in the sea, Brünhild reigns as supreme monarch, exceedingly strong, determined to assert her independence from, and superiority over, all suitors. There may be a parallel to be drawn between her and Kriemhild in this respect. Both are essentially isolated, both reject the usual ritual of wooing and courtship. In Kriemhild's case, the rejection is passive; in Brünhild's, it is blatantly provocative in nature, for potential suitors pay with their lives for their folly. One other thing links Brünhild to Kriemhild: this bellicose queen of the north is also endowed with a keen awareness of the significance of power and its trappings.

A question begs itself from the outset: why does Brünhild devise tests which are impossible for anyone but Siegfried to endure? Furthermore, were these tests established before or after Siegfried and Brünhild had become acquainted with one another? As we have seen above, there is evidence in the *Nibelungenlied* to support the theory that a prior liaison has existed between the two figures, although it has by no means been as intense as in the Nordic tradition (see Appendix A, particularly the *Völsunga Saga*). Does Brünhild consciously intend to "ward off" suitors until Siegfried returns? The text is left deliberately vague on this point, but when Brünhild is first informed that Siegfried may be among the wooing party, she assumes that he is the suitor. The rules are, however, as valid for him as for anyone else: "unt ist der starke Sîfrit     komen in diz lant / durch willen mîner minne,     ez gât im an den lîp. / ich fürhte in niht sô sêre,     daz ich werde sîn wîp" ("And if strong Siegfried has come to this land to woo me, he will risk his life in the process. I am not so intimidated by him that I would simply concede to becoming his wife," 416.2–4).

Brünhild is the victim of massive deceit practiced by Siegfried and Gunther. When she perceives Gunther to have won the competition, she immediately calls upon her men and relations to swear allegiance to the Burgundian king (466.3–4). At this point, she does not appear to entertain any doubts as to the validity of Gunther's claim on her, although it is clear that she is disappointed by the outcome (note 462.1 and 465.3). That Brünhild is angered over her defeat is indicative of the fact that she had never intended, or expected, to be made subordinate to a man, perhaps not even to Siegfried. But she adheres to the rules, something which neither Gunther nor Siegfried is inclined to do. Siegfried demonstrates particular callousness toward her:

> "Sô wol mich dirre maere,"     sprach Sîfrit der degen,
> "daz iuwer hôhverte     ist alsô hie gelegen,
> daz iemen lebet, der iuwer     meister müge sîn.
> nu sult ir, maget edele,     uns hinnen volgen an den Rîn." (474)

("I am happy to hear that your haughtiness has been laid to rest," said the warrior Siegfried, "and that there is someone who has proven to be your master. And now, noble woman, you will accompany us to the Rhine.")

The remark is totally uncalled for; it may be indicative of Siegfried's own *superbia,* as he was the one to defeat Brünhild.

Brünhild's Amazon-like existence on Isenstein may, however, be regarded as symptomatic of a particular type of self-exaltation and hubris. Her role as powerful queen and eligible spouse, together with the tests she had created for potential suitors, cannot help but provide a challenge for any knight who desires a bride of stature. Brünhild's habit of killing unsuccessful aspirants, an act inherently demonic in its nature, stamps her as a figure of the Other World. (We note the various occasions on which she is associated with the devil in the seventh *Aventiure.*) There can be no doubt that she displays *übermuot,* but is it any less than that demonstrated by the frailer male representatives of courtly society who aspire to woo her? What intrigues us about Brünhild is her position as a supernaturally strong queen who appears to have established herself as a formidable counterpart to an otherwise male-dominated world. This, in itself, is a remarkable illustration of what Theodore M. Andersson has called "the element of will."[29]

What really motivates Brünhild? A strong case can be made for her desire to achieve self-fulfillment, to assert constantly her penchant for independence. That this self-assertion has a dark side is clear from the text, but the poet is not prone to dwell upon it. For him, as for Gunther (and Siegfried), Brünhild is a magnificent prize, the epitome of royal stature and power, a queen and potential partner without equal. She is there to be conquered, although her removal from the Other World at Isenstein is fraught with peril.

If Brünhild had any doubts about the manner in which she had suffered defeat in the ordeals, this is not evident immediately. On the surface, at least, she has accepted the situation. Her suspicions are only aroused when the game of deceit played by Gunther and Siegfried is not adhered to consistently. When Kriemhild is allowed to sit next to Siegfried, the illusion of the latter as Gunther's vassal is immediately disrupted: "dô sah si Kriemhilde    (done wart ir nie sô leit) / bî Sîfride sitzen:    weinen si began" ("When she saw Kriemhild sitting next to Siegfried, Brünhild began to cry. She had never known such sorrow," 618.2–3). This is a point in the *Nibelungenlied* open to two interpretations: (1) Brünhild has a keenly

developed sense of social and courtly etiquette. The sight of a vassal
sitting next to the princess of a powerful ruling family, of which
she is about to become a member, is anathema to her. This is the
reason (or excuse?) she offers for her tears, claiming that it will
shame Kriemhild to be seen with a vassal (620; see also 622);
(2) Brünhild does, in fact, entertain feelings for Siegfried (which
are never expressed candidly) that cause her to weep when she sees
him obviously attracted to another woman. De Boor, in his commentary to strophe 620, has maintained that there is no necessity
to read latent jealousy into the queen's words, and, in this regard,
the text is on his side. While we can assume that there has been
some sort of contact between Brünhild and Siegfried prior to Gunther's wooing mission, there is no clear evidence to support the theory
that Brünhild, for her part, had felt strongly about the hero of
Xanten. She herself never displays any overt or covert signs of love
when around him. There are no "spaehe blicke" ("furtive glances"),
no smiles, no endearing exchange of words. As we have already
witnessed above, Siegfried behaves in a blatantly callous manner
toward Brünhild following her defeat in Iceland. The Scandinavian
tradition, however, portrayed Siegfried as an oath-breaker (see Appendix A), and the question will continue to be raised whether the
author of the *Nibelungenlied* did not have this tradition in mind when
he depicted the tearful Brünhild. However we may wish to view
Brünhild's reaction at this point, the most important function of
the scene is to draw attention to the fact that the queen's suspicions
have been aroused, leading her to deny Gunther her body, which,
in turn, brings her (albeit unknowingly) into a combative situation
with Siegfried once again; and this leads directly to her quarrel with
Kriemhild and, ultimately, Siegfried's death.

Brünhild's words: "ich wil noch magt belîben,     (ir sult wol
merken daz / unz ich diu maer' ervinde . . . " ("I shall remain a
virgin until I know the whole story, and you had better take note
of it," 635.3–4a) illustrate the intensity of her confusion and frus-
tration. The fact that she can overpower Gunther and leave him
hanging from a nail on the wall for the night (637ff.) cannot help
but strengthen her conviction that Gunther is withholding infor--
mation from her. The scene may be considered humorous by the
modern reader (and possibly by his medieval counterpart), but its
ramifications are of a decidedly serious nature. Can Brünhild's "defeat" (more precisely, "taming") at the hands of Siegfried (in his

magic cloak) alleviate her doubts? She has been divested of her supernatural powers, and now appears willing to grant Gunther her favors (678), but she has certainly found out nothing more about the "maere."

It continues to bother Brünhild that neither Siegfried nor Kriemhild behaves in a manner befitting vassals of her husband; it is, in fact, something she dwells on ("alle zîte," 724.1). Although Gunther has already told her that Siegfried is a king in his own right (623), he has done nothing to make it clear to Brünhild that the hero of Xanten is not his vassal. Viewed from Brünhild's perspective, there is sufficient reason to grow somewhat anxious over the lack of tangible service afforded Worms by Siegfried, and to wonder how Kriemhild who, having lowered herself through her marriage to a liegeman, could "carry her head so high" (724.2–3). By managing to have Siegfried and Kriemhild invited to Worms, Brünhild clearly wishes to force the issue. Both Gunther and Siegfried appear to be aware of the potential danger of a rendezvous in Worms (note 727 and 751.4), yet both acquiesce in the end.

While Brünhild may have been "tamed" by Siegfried and lost her superhuman strength, her "domestication" has done nothing to lessen her awareness of power and status within society. She is eager to learn how Siegfried, as Gunther's vassal, can enjoy such broad freedoms (from tribute, service, etc.) and independence, but Brünhild is also concerned about the prestige of her own husband and his land. She did not, after all, relinquish sovereignty over Iceland to become queen to someone who is second-rate. Gunther must be the foremost of all kings, for he alone was able to best her in the ordeals and in bed. It is, therefore, to be expected that her reaction to Kriemhild's (by no means harmless) remark that Siegfried should rule over all the (Burgundian) lands (815.3–4) emphasizes Gunther's primacy as a monarch: "die wîle lebt Gunther,    sô kundez nimmer ergân" ("As long as Gunther is alive, that cannot come about," 816.4). Kriemhild's assertion that Siegfried is Gunther's "genôz" ("equal," 819.4) must add to Brünhild's confusion, but hearing her declare him to be even "tiwerr" ("superior," 824.2) to the Burgundian monarch arouses her fury: "Du ziuhest dich ze hôhe" ("You are going too far," 826.1). At this point, Brünhild is less concerned with learning more about Siegfried's enigmatic status vis-à-vis Gunther than she is with asserting herself over Kriemhild. One has the impression, however, that a curtain is being raised slowly before her eyes, and that elements of the massive deceit practiced against her are gradually coming into view. The producing of the ring (847.2) and the girdle (849.3) in public serves as irrefutable evidence of the validity of Kriemhild's claim that Siegfried had made love to Brünhild before she had ever been together with Gunther (840.2–3).

Once the events which have transpired before the minster are reported to Gunther, Hagen, and the others, Brünhild's function within the epic has effectively come to an end. She is no longer accorded any active role in the succeeding *Aventiuren*. Siegfried's alleged boasting of having bedded Brünhild—now common knowledge, even if he is ready to deny it under oath—has brought dishonor to both Brünhild and the Burgundian royal house. She herself realizes that Siegfried was the one who overcame her and appears to believe that he may, in fact, have robbed her of her virginity. Her marriage to Gunther is a sham, as it must follow that Siegfried was also responsible for her defeat during the ordeals in Iceland. He is the one who should have become her husband. In the following *Aventiuren,* we are granted only fleeting glimpses of the queen. The message seems clear: Brünhild's fate was ultimately linked to that of Siegfried. Once Siegfried disappears from the epic, Brünhild's existence becomes essentially irrelevant. Thematically, one might go so far as to say that she "dies" with Siegfried. With the knowledge that she has been totally deceived, and that most of the court, if not all of it, suspects that she has had a much more intimate liaison with Siegfried, Brünhild is relegated to a position of spiritual isolation much more intense than the physical isolation in which she is depicted as queen of Iceland. Deprived of her dignity, power, and any possibility of happiness, she is destined to live out a weary existence as queen of Burgundy, a life to which even her son, Siegfried (see 718), is incapable of restoring a sense of productivity.

## Chapter Three
# Kings and Vassals
## The Ruling Kings: Gunther, Siegmund, Attila

Gunther, Siegmund, Attila: one thing binds them together beyond their claim to sovereignty, namely, their helplessness when it is a question of controlling events and preventing catastrophes. Given their positions, no figures in the *Nibelungenlied* appear more paradoxically cast than these three. Had the poet been intent upon offering through them a categorical condemnation of kingship, or of demonstrating what kings must not be like, he could hardly have improved upon his models. Confronted with situations which threaten to wreak havoc in their respective worlds, they show themselves to be either naive or impotent, or even unwitting collaborators in bringing about the destruction that follows.

**Gunther.** Had Gunther taken a firm stand against Siegfried when confronted by the latter's arrogance in the initial arrival scene in Worms, he might have lost his life then and there, but this, at least, would have spared him depiction as a royal incompetent, a king without answers, a monarch constantly overshadowed by others, including his liegemen. Throughout the *Nibelungenlied,* one has the distinct impression that Gunther is leader of the Burgundians in name only, that he cannot be placed on the same level with Siegfried or his vassal Hagen. Was the poet simply toying with his audience when he referred to Gunther as "ein riter wolgetân" ("a fine and noble knight," 328.2), whose "grimme[r] . . . muot" ("irascible nature," 142.4) gives cause to consternation on the part of Liudeger's and Liudegast's envoys in the fourth *Aventiure?* On what is their fear based? Hearsay? Truth? The reputation of Gunther's vassals, particularly Hagen? We may be willing to grant that, at some time in the past, Gunther did, in fact, acquire a name for himself through personal exploits. What we see of him in the *Nibelungenlied,* however, at least until the concluding *Aventiuren,* is scarcely evidence of his ability to lead the Burgundian nation. His weaknesses and his mistakes can be summed up as follows: (1) his

far too conciliatory nature when initially confronted by Siegfried;
(2) his total dependence on the latter in the wooing and taming of
Brünhild, a woman totally unsuited to be his spouse (a fact that he
recognizes, but that his *übermuot* prevents him from accepting);
(3) his less than resolute or consistent stance in the matter of Siegfried's murder; (4) a cavalier attitude toward all the wrongs done
his sister Kriemhild; (5) his total lack of insight with respect to the
significance of Kriemhild's marriage to Attila as well as the invitation extended the Burgundians to visit her husband's court; (6) his
repeated ignoring of crystal-clear indications of what is to befall not
only himself, but also the Burgundian people.

On the other side of this "balance sheet" we may cite the bearing
demonstrated by Gunther when the catastrophe is upon him, his
unswerving loyalty to Hagen, and his heroism in the face of death.
Yet, even here, Gunther seems to remain remarkably unaware of
the full ramifications of the slaughter in Attila's Great Hall. The
Burgundian warrior class is wiped out; for all intents and purposes,
the deaths of Gunther, Hagen, and all those who have followed
them to Hungary signify the end of Burgundy as a political entity.
Gunther may depart the world a "guoter ritter lîp" ("a good knight,"
2364.2), as he is referred to by his adversary Dietrich, but one
cannot help wondering whether greater decisiveness and a more
stalwart character in the earlier part of the epic might not have
prevented matters from getting so much out of hand.

It is, of course, not simply Gunther's lack of decisiveness which
proves to have fatal consequences for both himself and countless
others, but also his inability to accept his own limitations, in a
word, his *übermuot*. This is what motivates him to woo and marry
Brünhild, and it also precludes any revealing, on his part, to Attila
of the true circumstances that prevail at the Hunnish court (see
1865.4). He is not entirely unaware that he has such limitations,
as is clear from the anxiety he expresses in strophe 442, after he
has watched three men struggle to bring Brünhild's spear to her:
"waz sol diz wesen? / der tiuvel ûz der helle    wie kund'er dâ vor
genesen?" ("What will the outcome be? How could even the devil
survive this?" 442.1–2). But he lacks the insight or (instinct) to
pull back, to realize that he is totally out of place here. He gives
in to the "Sinnendämon"[1] ("the demon of lust") and at no time
reflects on the possible consequences of concluding a royal marriage
based on deceit. In essence, Gunther is controlled by his narcissism;

and, in this regard, he is very different from Hagen. While one cannot contend that the latter never evinces personal motives for his actions, his primary concern is Burgundy and the status of the Burgundian kingdom. When Gunther chooses to pursue Brünhild, he has only himself in mind. In his relationship to Siegfried, Gunther would like to establish and retain a good rapport with the latter. Unlike Hagen, however, he does not perceive the potential danger which Siegfried represents for the Burgundian court, possibly through his very existence. It is in keeping with his nature, for Gunther is oblivious to the ultimate significance of numerous events in the *Nibelungenlied,* including the excessive lamenting of his sister over the death of Siegfried. He is warned by Hagen, Ute, and Rumold not to accept the invitation to go to Hungary; yet he defies their advice. Even when he and the other Burgundians are told by Hagen about the prophecy of the water sprite, he does not seem consistently cognizant of what lies in store for them. He appears to abandon his awareness of such ill portents during the festivities in both Bechelaren and at the court of Attila. At the conclusion of the work, he knows that he is doomed, but he goes to his death unaware of the full extent which he, in his impotent state, has helped to generate.

Siegmund. As Siegfried's father, Siegmund represents, in his maturity and worldly wisdom, a contrast to his son. How very correctly he warns Siegfried of the Burgundian court (53.4) and, in particular, of Hagen (54). Siegmund's anxiety centers around Siegfried's intention to procure Kriemhild as his bride and the danger his son may face at Worms as a result. The perilous wooing expedition is, of course, a popular topos in medieval literature, but the worry expressed by Siegmund does serve to establish, from the outset, a basic dichotomy between Xanten and Worms or between Siegfried and the Burgundians. One point may strike the reader as strange: is Siegmund not aware of his son's special powers, of the fact that he has already fought against supernatural creatures in the Other World? This would be odd, given the fact that Siegfried's youthful adventures were known in Worms before Siegfried set foot there. If one assumes that Siegmund is only too aware of his son's capabilities, then one might ask whether it is not precisely this which worries him. Siegfried is given to brash behavior, something which could prove problematical for society in general. Siegmund may know about Siegfried's near-invulnerability, but he quite possibly senses that his son may be led to tempt fate once too often; and Worms is clearly a place where, in his opinion, trouble could easily be stirred up. He does little to prevent Siegfried from undertaking the journey, however, and his initial warning tends to be scarcely more than tokenism.

In the *Nibelungenlied* we encounter the naive (Siegfried, Gunther, to some degree Kriemhild), the knowing (Hagen, the water sprite), and those who exhibit a sense of foreboding. To this latter category, which also includes figures such as Ute and Rumold, belongs Siegmund. On the night of his son's murder, he sleeps uneasily, and the narrator comments: "ich waene sîn herze im sagte,      daz im was geschehen: / er'n möhte sinen lieben sun      nimmer lebendic gesehen" ("I believe he knew in his heart what had happened. He would never see his beloved son alive again," 1016.3–4). What he has perceived as possible, even predicted in a more general sense, has come to pass. Could he have been more instrumental in preventing it? Siegmund might well have become more actively engaged on behalf of his son, for he had clearly entertained doubts about Worms for some time. But while he was happy to watch Siegfried bask in the splendor of knighthood, to support him in every endeavor, his relationship to his son does not strike us as being particularly profound. What Siegfried needed most upon returning from the Other World was a mentor similar to Hrothgar in *Beowulf*, who advises the hero, after the latter has destroyed the Other World monsters, to be wary of pride and arrogance.[2] In this respect, Siegmund fails as a father, and his lack of decisiveness leads to the loss of that which he holds most dear. As if to underscore this basic weakness, Siegmund returns to Xanten following Siegfried's murder without having raised his sword to avenge it. Nor does he ever return to Worms to demand justice. He also resigns himself to Kriemhild's decision not to accompany him. As Kriemhild simultaneously elects to abandon her son, Gunther, Siegmund will assume the role of the latter's protector and educator. But there is no indication in the text that he gains any solace from this function. When he disappears from the *Nibelungenlied,* he does so as "ein ganz und gar Vereinsamter" ("totally alone and isolated").[3]

Attila.    He was modeled after one of the most successful warrior kings of all times, a ruler who, by the time of his death in 453, had brought much of Europe under his sway. While the historical Attila is often referred to as the scourge of God, the Attila (Etzel) of the *Nibelungenlied* is portrayed in a much more benevolent light, a revered potentate to both heathen and Christian alike, and a man of sufficient stature to command the allegiance of figures such as Dietrich and Rüdeger. Deeply concerned with prestige, harmony, and productivity within his realm, Attila's primary aim in marrying Kriemhild following the death of Queen Helche is to restore general confidence and the belief in a productive future (through the promise of progeny), although he is also eager to procure for himself a woman of the beauty and fame associated with Siegfried's widow.

Attila's weakness lies in his inability to distinguish between reality and appearance. Like his Burgundian counterpart, Gunther, he is unaware of the deeper significance of Kriemhild's actions. Years of abject sorrow spent by the queen are only too apparent to Hagen while she resides in Worms, and do not go unnoticed by Dietrich in Hungary (note 1724.4). Yet neither monarch appears to notice a thing. The dichotomy between illusion and reality is never more poignantly demonstrated than in the person of Attila. He has no idea of the machinations of his wife, of the fate she plans for the Burgundians (1754.2–3), of her confrontation with Hagen. (One might suggest that Dietrich was imprudent in not advising Attila of the true state of affairs.) Although Hagen may be depicted as Attila's friend (1757.2), it is hardly possible that the Hunnish king should be unaware of the fact that the hero of Troneck is also the murderer of Siegfried. It is common knowledge among his men (1733). For Attila, time appears to have relativized the murder. He is thus easily deceived by Kriemhild into believing that she is content with her life as queen of the Hunnish Empire, and at no time does he entertain the thought that he may be but another instrument in her effort to exact revenge.

Attila is, in essence, a pathetic figure. His court becomes the scene of one confrontation after another between Kriemhild and Hagen, of escalating tensions between the Burgundians and factions among the Huns. Yet, Attila sees nothing. His blindness with respect to the significance of events transpiring around him contributes to the death of his son Ortlieb at the hands of Hagen, although the latter had already made an ominous reference to the prince's fate in strophe 1918: "doch ist der künec junge  sô veiclîch getân" ("However, the young prince is fated to die").

Isolated from Kriemhild, Attila exhibits qualities of the "ideal" ruler: he is noble, powerful, tolerant. His desire to woo Kriemhild

is based on the laudable premise that he and his people would regain
happiness through the acquisition of a queen. However, he fails to
comprehend that Kriemhild's reason for marrying him is not productive in nature, and that this union is destined to bring his very
empire to its knees, for Kriemhild has already degenerated to a point
where she no longer feels bound by courtly mores.

That a catastrophe of such magnitude should befall Attila is
evidence of the fact that he no longer controls matters in a manner
one might expect of a ruler. He certainly feels obliged to avenge
the death of Ortlieb, but the reader is not given the impression that
he is actually in command during the fighting against the Burgundians. When Gunther and Hagen are finally captured by Dietrich,
they are turned over to Kriemhild, not to Attila. It is not until
Hagen is struck down by Kriemhild that Attila seems to understand
what has actually transpired: "wie ist nu tôt gelegen / von eines
wîbes handen   der aller beste degen, / der ie kom ze sturme   oder
ie schilt getruoc!" ("Now the best warrior who ever fought in battle,
who ever bore a shield, has been killed by a woman!" 2374.1–3).
It is a man's world, and here, at least, cameraderie among enemies
is not lacking: "swie vîent ich im waere,   ez ist mir leide genuoc"
("However much I was his enemy, this causes me great sorrow,"
2374.4). Attila's remarks are all the more noteworthy when one
considers how Hagen had mocked him when he was forced to leave
the Great Hall under the protection of Dietrich (2023). Attila sur-
vives the carnage as the sovereign of a people totally devastated; in
contrast, it is his queen, Kriemhild, who, although she does not
survive, proves to be the more sovereign individual, albeit in a
negative sense.

## Dietrich and Rüdeger

Both Dietrich and Rüdeger have been regarded as representatives
of "Christian knighthood" in the *Nibelungenlied*.[4] On the surface,
the image of both figures presented by the author is positive. In a
world gone berserk, they appear to be the only personalities of stature
to retain a measure of dignity. Bert Nagel has referred to Dietrich's
victory over Hagen and Gunther as one of "superior morality,"[5] and
to the person himself as "the bearer of chivalrous Christianity."[6]
But is Dietrich, in fact, to be understood as chivalry's response to
the "excesses of old, heathen heroism?"[7] Does the figure represent
a basic norm by which new ethical standards can be determined?

Dietrich is a great and widely respected leader in his own right, and there is no lack of textual evidence to support a predominantly positive interpretation of his character. But what are we to make of the friendly manner in which he greets, and simultaneously warns, Hagen and the others of Kriemhild's continued grief (1724)? Does Dietrich condone Siegfried's murder? At no time are we given any indication of how Dietrich feels toward Siegfried; but it is, perhaps, still possible to draw some conclusions concerning his sentiments about the long-dead hero. From the moment Dietrich learns of the Burgundians' arrival in Hungary, he is distressed: "ez was im harte leit" ("He was very unhappy about it," 1718.3b; see also 1723.3b and 1750.4). Dietrich senses that nothing good can come of it, because he is fully aware of the animosity which Kriemhild still perceives toward the Burgundians. He and Hagen appear to be the only figures who truly comprehend the level of Kriemhild's depravity, and it is this which prompts Dietrich to warn the guests. Is it a laudable act? In one sense, it is certainly that, for the Burgundians are the invited guests of Attila and, as such, can expect to enjoy immunity from attack or harassment while in his domain. Dietrich may not know what Kriemhild is planning, but he suspects the queen of treachery and feels a moral (as well as a "comradely") obligation to inform the Burgundians of the true state of affairs. But this must be predicated on the belief that Siegfried's murder is not worth avenging after such a long period of time, or, perhaps, that it was justified in the first place. He, for one, has no intention of calling Hagen to task for it (note 1902.4).

Yet, if Dietrich is to be lauded for forewarning the Burgundians, one may be less inclined to side with him when he labels Kriemhild a "vâlandinne" (1748.4a) in public. This is not because there is any doubt that the queen has degenerated into something less than a human being even at this point, but rather because Dietrich's lack of sensitivity cannot help but force her into even greater isolation. Seen from Kriemhild's (albeit tortured) perspective, no one has stepped forward to take her side in the matter of Siegfried's death or the "theft" of the Nibelung treasure. Dietrich may well condemn Kriemhild's harping for revenge long after she has remarried, but what is to be gained by insulting her publicly? If he perceives the extent of her grief correctly, as seems to be the case, how could he believe that castigation of this sort, in the very presence of her enemy, can do anything to temper her wrath?

As perceptive as he is, Dietrich must realize that the king of the Huns is not cognizant of his wife's machinations. As the situation becomes steadily worse, the reader is inclined to ask why he does not simply inform Attila of Kriemhild's intentions. After having upbraided the queen in the twenty-eighth *Aventiure,* Dietrich disappears into the background until he is needed again in the thirty-third *Aventiure* to escort Attila and Kriemhild out of the Great Hall. This is highly significant when we attempt to construct a "total" picture of the leader of the Amelungs. He remains relatively passive, allowing events which he seems to have anticipated to unfold without making the slightest effort to check them before they get out of hand. Dietrich is a great warrior, respected by Burgundians and Huns alike, and feared by Kriemhild (1749.2), but he is no statesman. Timely intervention on his part might have prevented the slaughter which followed, but there is no appeal to reason, no expression of faith uttered by him that all will turn out for the better. He may express some consternation about his own welfare once fighting has broken out in the Great Hall (1984.2), but the reader cannot avoid the impression that he is in his element, even though he may not yet draw his sword against the Burgundians. Once out of the Hall, he withdraws for yet another five *Aventiuren,* in accordance with his assurance of peace to the Burgundians as he leaves the scene of the fighting. It is only when he learns of Rüdeger's death (2245) that his mood begins to change, and not until he discovers that all of his men save Hildebrand have been killed does he decide to go into battle against Hagen and Gunther. It should be noted, however, that his motives are basically self-centered. The Burgundians, by wiping out his men, have caused him the greatest injury possible on this earth (2319.1), because there is no one left to help him establish his rule in "Amelunge lant" (2322.4; see also 2330.3–4 and 2332.3–4).[8]

There is no room for any Christianity here. Dietrich, in a lament which reminds one of the despair perceived by the young Parzival, even maintains "sô hât mîn got vergezzen" ("Then God has forsaken me," 2319.3). His behavior at the conclusion of the epic is indeed enigmatic. He offers Gunther and Hagen assurance of safe passage home if they give themselves up to him (2337 and 2340), but once he has captured them, he turns them over to Kriemhild with merely a request that they not be mistreated (2355 and 2364). Immediately thereafter, he again moves into the background, leaving Hagen and

Gunther to their fate. Given the degree of perception demonstrated by Dietrich earlier, his disposition of Hagen and Gunther seems incomprehensible. In a sense, he, too, has fallen victim to Kriemhild's machinations. It is clearly she whom he regards as the de facto leader of the Huns.

Dietrich is no more a representative of "Christian knighthood" than is Hagen. His main concern is to establish a new empire with his Amelungs, and thus he is primarily self-oriented. This is why he remains neutral so long while the slaughter goes on about him.[9] Dietrich does not embody any "new spirit," nor does he represent a sign of hope for the future.[10] He is caught up in events just like everyone else and may justifiably be criticized for the indelicate manner in which he contributes to furthering Kriemhild's isolation. Dietrich is a great warrior in a physical sense, but he shares with all the other figures a marked incapacity to govern events. In this regard, he is a victim of fate, not its master.

Rüdeger, margrave of Bechelaren, a place described by Friedrich Panzer as an "Idyll,"[11] is the figure most frequently associated with the courtly world and Christianity. In the service of the heathen Attila, he travels as envoy to the Burgundian court, and it is his oath of fealty to Kriemhild (1255) which prompts the queen to consent to the marriage with Attila. But it is also this oath which, recalled later by Kriemhild, leads to the moral and legal predicament faced by Rüdeger when hostilities break out between Huns and Burgundians.

As is the case with so many other figures in the *Nibelungenlied,* Rüdeger appears oblivious to the true state of affairs. Just how much does he know of Kriemhild's intentions? Dietrich had assumed that Rüdeger had insight into the queen's frame of mind and that he would have forewarned the Burgundians during their stay at Bechelaren (note 1723.4). But Rüdeger seems to know, or at least suspect, nothing. He is, after all, somewhat isolated from Attila's court. Both he and his wife Gotelind accord the Burgundians generous hospitality (see 1646). Panzer's description of Bechelaren as an "Idyll" seems, on the surface, to be quite appropriate. The Burgundians enter a world of courtly refinement and harmony. As we have already witnessed with Dietrich, the greeting extended to Hagen by Rüdeger is particularly enthusiastic (1657.3). There is no reference, either in private or in public, to a potentially dangerous situation. In fact, portents of a positive and productive future pre-

vail, and Rüdeger supports Hagen's suggestion that Giselher be
betrothed to his daughter. Hagen himself is given the shield of
Nuodung, a relative of Gotelind (1700–1701).

The rapport between Rüdeger and the Burgundians is calculated
to heighten the tragedy which ensues when Rüdeger is forced to go
into combat against his former guests. As with Siegfried, there are
aspects of Rüdeger's character which make him a problematical
figure. Ihlenburg is probably correct to express reservations about
Gottfried Weber's designation of Rüdeger as the "ambitious cour-
tier".[12] There can be no question of the seriousness with which
Rüdeger considers his personal honor,[13] but it is difficult to support
the idea that he is, at least in the modern sense of the word, an
opportunist. The oath which he swears to Kriemhild undoubtedly
pertains, from his perspective, to the avenging of any injustice that
might befall the queen, but it is remarkable that in his effort to
accord the margrave predominantly positive character traits, the
poet allowed him to appear so wanting in his judgment of character.

Rüdeger finds himself in a much greater predicament than that
faced by Dietrich. He has guided the Burgundians to the court of
Attila, and thus feels bound not to engage in the fighting against
them:

> "Unde allez daz ich möhte,      daz het ich in getân,
> niwan daz ich die recken      her gefüeret hân.
> jâ was ich ir geleite      in mînes herren lant;
> des ensol mit in niht strîten      mîn vil ellendes hant." (2144)

("I would have done everything I could to cause them injury, had I not
been the one to bring them here. But I was the one who led them into
my lord's country and, for this reason, I may not lift my wretched hand
against them.")

Rüdeger's honor and a sense of legal obligation bind him to the
Burgundians, but his oaths of fealty bind him to Attila and Kriemhild. When reminded by Kriemhild of the oath he swore to her
(2149), Rüdeger declares that he had taken no oath to sell his soul:
"daz ich die sêle vliese,      des enhân ich niht gesworn" (2150.3).
The reference to "sêle" may appear to lend support to an interpretation of Rüdeger as a figure whose actions are largely motivated
by Christianity. Actually, however, Rüdeger is more concerned

about the loss of his honor in this world than he is about the loss
of his immortal soul:

"Owê mir gotes armen,     daz ich dize gelebet hân.
aller mîner êren     der muoz ich abe stân,
triuwen unde zühte,     der got an mir gebôt.
owê got von himele,     daz michs niht wendet der tôt!" (2153)

("Alas, that I must witness this, Godforsaken man that I am. Now I shall
have to relinquish all of my honor (respect), my integrity, and my breeding,
which I have been granted by God. Alas, God in Heaven, that death does
not prevent me from having to suffer it!")

Either Rüdeger uses "sêle" without according it any real religious
depth, or the term is, in this case, simply a euphemism for *êre*.[14]

The entire,thirty-seventh *Aventiure* is devoted to a description of
Rüdeger's plight, his subsequent battle against the Burgundians,
and his death. It is a part of the epic which has received many
interpretations, most of which center around the question of the
margrave's honor as well as the problem of whether or not his death
is tragic. Rüdeger is regarded as the one figure among both Burgundians and Huns who finds himself in a moral and religious
dilemma,[15] forced to choose between two possible courses of action,
each of which, he feels, will cost him his honor. This scene—the
hero torn between two equally problematical decisions—has been
cited as an indication of just how "Germanic" the *Nibelungenlied* can
be.[16]

From a legal standpoint, Rüdeger's position is clear. As a liegeman
of Attila, he is duty-bound to attack his king's enemies, even though
he may feel that to do so will compromise his honor. Are his fears
in this respect justified? Rüdeger proclaims to the Burgundians that
he is obliged by oath to fight them (2178.2). The latter make every
effort to dissuade him, but on no occasion do they infer that Rüdeger
will be any less honorable, at least in their eyes, for fulfilling his
legal commitment. One has the distinct impression that they fully
comprehend the plight in which the margrave finds himself. Hagen,
in particular, recognizes that Rüdeger is a man of dignity, that he
has obviously reflected deeply on the significance of what he is legally
bound to do, and that he is inwardly torn apart by the decision to
fight the Burgundians. In a very real sense, Rüdeger is also a victim

of Kriemhild's unrelenting passion for revenge, and Hagen perceives an affinity toward him which transcends even the mutual respect opponents may entertain for one another.

Commenting on Rüdeger's generosity toward Hagen in this situation, Mowatt and Sacker claim somewhat cynically:

There seems to be something pathetically inadequate about everything Rüdeger has to offer. It is as if he tries to cover up the primitive basis of relationships by typing people around him as recognizably innocuous members of society. . . . [T]he inheritor of his sword is not necessarily his friend for life. With Hagen he does manage to make a private agreement, a sort of two-man society, but their truce has no effect on their eventual fate. [17]

One cannot help but feel that such an interpretation of Rüdeger's generosity is unjustifiably anachronistic. Rüdeger gives sincerely. When he presents his shield to Hagen in the Great Hall, it is a symbolic gesture of the inner affinity he feels toward the man. The fact that "their truce has no effect on their eventual fate" did not concern the poet, whose wish seems to have been to portray two warriors whom fate had cast on opposite sides, but who, nonetheless, establish and retain a bond between themselves which extends beyond that of convention. Hagen and Rüdeger are destined to die, but not at each other's hands. They thus transcend the ultimate fate brought upon them by Kriemhild's machinations. Objectively, it may be noted that Rüdeger has brought much of the dilemma he faces upon himself by swearing an oath thirteen years earlier somewhat precipitately.

Rüdeger dies in combat against Gernot (2220), who also perishes. Furthermore, all of the margrave's knights die at the hands of the Burgundians. But there is no loss of honor. Rüdeger is mourned as deeply as Gernot by the Burgundians (2223.3; see also 2225). They appear to have understood completely the situation in which Rüdeger found himself, and that his decision to enter the fray was made only after long reflection, and then with a heavy heart. The poet presents a striking contrast between the spirit of camaraderie embodied by the Burgundians toward their fallen opponent and the callous attitude of Kriemhild toward Rüdeger, whom she suspects of having attempted to reach a settlement with the former: "der helt hât missetân. / der uns dâ solde rechen,    der wil der suone pflegen" ("The knight has betrayed us. Instead of avenging us, as he ought to, he is attempting to bring about a reconciliation," 2229.2b–3).

Rüdeger displays some of the naiveté we have already encountered in Siegfried. In his case, however, the tragic ramifications of the precipitate oath remain concentrated in his own person. He is also different from Siegfried in one very noteworthy way. While Rüdeger may feel that he is in a hopeless situation, a kind of spiritual isolation,[18] he enjoys the respect and sympathy of those against whom he must fight, foremost among them, Hagen, who even refuses to raise his sword against him. Such sentiments are totally lacking on the part of the Burgundians toward Siegfried.

## Volker

What did the poet intend with Volker, *Spielmann* and warrior at one and the same time? Was he, with his awareness of the darker side of human existence, to represent the antithesis of the *Minnesänger,* a type of sober realist, as has been cautiously suggested by Gottfried Weber?[19] There can be little doubt that Volker has nothing to do with the finer image of the courtly knight, that he is made of more primitive stuff. But it would seem that there is less of an effort made to portray him as the opposite of a predominant artist-type of the time than as the positive representative of Germanic *triuwe.* Whatever one may think of Volker, it is impossible to conceive of him without considering the special relationship he enjoys with Hagen.

When Hagen and Dietrich take leave of each other in the twenty-ninth *Aventiure,* Hagen immediately looks "über ahsel" ("over his shoulder," 1758.3) in what can be interpreted as an effort to "seek out," at least optically, someone on whom he can rely during the ordeal to follow. The friendship with Volker which evolves is unique in the poem. Hagen may have chosen Volker for his martial skills, which, as his performance during the subsequent fighting illustrates, are indeed considerable, as well as for his "grimmen muot" ("irascible nature," 1759.3), but it is soon evident that the two enjoy a "spiritual" bond unparalleled in the *Nibelungenlied.* They are referred to metaphorically as "tier diu wilden" ("wild animals," 1762.1) by the Huns, and their alliance causes Kriemhild considerable distress (1762.4), for she is aware of Volker's reputation as an "übel man" ("rough fellow," 1768.3).

Volker is the only Burgundian other than Hagen who remains consistently cognizant of the true state of affairs and who acts accordingly. His immediate acquiesence to Hagen's request that he stand by him is based on respect for the hero of Troneck and on his awareness that his honor will allow him to do no different. When Volker refers to "vriunt Hagene" ("friend Hagen") in 1773.1 and 1774.1 the repetition of the appellative underscores its sincerity, and it is reciprocated by Hagen in 1777.1. Hagen may be arrogant, ruthless, and calculating, but, unlike Siegfried, he does not become spiritually and physically isolated from the rest of society. His stature is such that he is able to command both the respect and admiration of friend and enemy alike. Nowhere in the epic can one find a firmer declaration of unqualified support for or loyalty toward a friend than in Volker's response to Hagen's appeal for assistance:

"Ich hilf' iu sicherlîchen,"     sprach der spileman,
"ob ich uns engegene saehe     den künec selben gân
mit allen sînen recken.     die wîle ich leben muoz,
so entwîch' ich iu durch vorhte     ûz helfe nimmer einen fuoz." (1778)


("Of course I will help you," the fiddler said, "and even if I should see the king advancing toward us with all of his warriors, as long as I am alive, I will not be frightened into reneging an instant on the assistance I have promised you.")


Volker provides both physical and spiritual consolation to Hagen at a moment when the latter may well have felt himself in danger of becoming isolated.

Volker had no part in Siegfried's murder (although, like everyone else, he knows that it was Hagen who killed the hero), nor does he entertain any personal animosity toward Kriemhild. (We may note 1780, where he even recommends that they rise in her presence.) His alliance with Hagen is based on what he would consider to be the *triuwe* owed a fellow warrior in time of peril.

Volker is portrayed as both a warrior and a musician whose melodies can serve to uplift spirits (1835) and also lull the Burgundians to sleep (1836). He is as proficient with the bow as he is with the sword, but it is his prowess as a warrior which is accorded the most attention. In contrast to Hagen, however, whose actions are normally predicated on considerable deliberation, Volker appears as something of a hothead, ready to give pursuit to a band of timid Huns (1842), although, as Hagen prudently points out, this could place their sleeping comrades in danger (1844). It is the *Spielmann* who commits the first "open" act of hostility against the Huns by felling a "trût der vrouwen" ("lady's man," 1886.2) among the Hunnish jousting party (1889). As strophes 1893–95 demonstrate, the situation is extremely critical, and an outbreak of hostilities between the Burgundians and Huns is only prevented by the timely (but also naive) intervention of Attila (1896–97).

Volker is not a person given to procrastination when it is a question of settling an issue. He would prefer to "get on with it," to have the Burgundians and Huns come to grips as soon as possible, since he knows that a fight is unavoidable. In battle, Volker is in his element, and the poet cannot refrain from portraying him in a somewhat humorous vein as he "fiddles" his way with a sword through Attila's Great Hall in the thirty-third *Aventiure* (note 1976ff.). When Volker is finally struck down by Hildebrand in the thirty-eighth *Aventiure,* the loss perceived by Hagen is indicative of the esteem which the *Spielmann* had enjoyed as a warrior and comrade: "Dô sach von Tronege Hagene    Volkêren tôt. / daz was zer hôhgezîte    sîn aller meistiu nôt, / die er dâ hete gewunnen    an mâgen und ouch an man" ("Then Hagen of Troneck saw Volker lying there dead. That was the greatest loss he had suffered at this 'festival,' whether in regard to friends or relatives" 2289.1–3).

## Gernot and Giselher

Neither Gernot nor Giselher, as brothers of both Gunther and Kriemhild (in their own right, kings, but within the feudal hierarchy, subordinate to Gunther), are individuals who rise above events, who are endowed with foresight or any outstanding ability as statesmen. To be sure, Gernot is to be credited with having prevented Hagen's nephew, Ortwin, from engaging Siegfried in combat during the initial arrival scene at Worms (119.4), and he makes an appeal to settle their differences "mit zühten" ("in a courtly or civilized manner," 120.3), but he and his brother acquiesce in the murder of Siegfried, and are ineffective, and, perhaps, even hypocritical in their "efforts" to protect their sister from further "affronts" on the part of Hagen.

Giselher opposes the suggestion that Siegfried be killed (866). Gernot, although he voices no opinion at this point, does not appear to agree to the scheme, but we should note that he does not raise any formal protest against Ortwin's declaration that he would be prepared to deal with Siegfried if Gunther would but give the word (869.2–3). One cannot escape the impression that Giselher and Gernot are, in the final analysis, prepared to allow events to take their course. They may regret the murder once it has been committed, but there is never any indication that they are inclined to undertake measures to prevent it. By emphasizing the role of Hagen and Gunther in the act, particularly that of the former, the poet either intentionally or unintentionally directs the attention of his reader away from Giselher and Gernot, allowing them, in this instance, to assume the position of "by-standers," almost indistinguishable from the scores of knights and squires who later participate in the "hunt." In strophe 1097, Gernot may exclaim to Siegmund that he is innocent of the murder of Siegfried, but his words ring hollow.

Gernot's plea to Kriemhild that she has lamented Siegfried's death too long (1110.2), together with Giselher's "vlêhen" ("entreaties," 1112.4), may set the stage for a reconciliation between Kriemhild and her brothers (Hagen is, of course, omitted), but all of this means very little when the trio conveniently "leaves town," allowing Hagen to sink Kriemhild's treasure in the Rhine. Their assertion that Hagen has acted very badly (1139) is, at best, pathetic. (Note, in particular, 1134, where Gernot suggests that they ought to have sunk it in the Rhine.) This entire episode may be considered somewhat vague (see de Boor's note to 1132ff.), but it appears abundantly clear that neither Gernot nor Giselher is prepared to do more than offer an ineffective and possibly feigned verbal protest for the travesty committed against their sister. Actually, Hagen is the only one who acts with complete, if ruthless, consistency. By removing the treasure, he has also eradicated a threat to the Burgundian court (as well as to himself).

By refusing to take an active role on behalf of their sister, Gernot and Giselher help to drive Kriemhild into greater isolation and, consequently, alienation from her own family. She may still demonstrate a certain affection toward them, particularly Giselher, in the second half of the epic, but nothing indicates more poignantly where their sentiments lie than when they refuse to have anything to do with turning over Hagen to Kriemhild in order to save themselves and the other Burgundians (see 2105–6). Paradoxically, while their inactivity in the first half of the *Nibelungenlied* might be interpreted as a manifestation of the *untriuwe* demonstrated toward Siegfried, they are now depicted as the epitome of the loyal comrades-in-arms. As was the case with their brother, Gunther, our impressions of Gernot and Giselher will tend to vary depending on what section of the epic we happen to be concerned with. Objectively, however, the human failings of both brothers contribute to the work's cataclysmic conclusion.

# Chapter Four
# Style and Structure

## Style

Simple, even dry; succinct to the point of being unclear; enigmatically contemplative; firm and powerful; despite its incredible intensity, full of reserve; adhering intentionally to the common where one senses a need for the highest form of expression; exaggerated only in its (almost persistent) moderation; gravely objective, and yet, despite its serious tenor, not without a certain subtlety, irony, and biting satire; sensitive, without ever becoming affected; sensuous, but seldom boorish; emotional, but never overly sentimental; not particularly euphuistic, and yet always pertinent, wherever possible replacing words with signs, looks, silence, acts— that is the style of the Nibelungenlied![1]

As the quotation from Timm demonstrates, any attempt to characterize the style of the *Nibelungenlied* succinctly must prove fruitless. In the presentation of his tale, the poet used various techniques and rhetorical devices, some to great effect, others with less success. There is, of course, no universal method for investigating style,[2] and there are particular difficulties involved in this process when one deals with the *Nibelungenlied*. The question arises as to whether the poet was indebted to an older tradition with respect not only to his subject matter, but also to the form in which that material was presented. Furthermore, the *Nibelungenlied* contains elements which demonstrate an affinity to genres other than heroic epic. Bert Nagel has maintained that while the plot of the work justifies its classification as an heroic epic, the atmosphere which prevails, especially toward the conclusion, underscores the elegiac character of the poem, and its "milieu descriptions" point in the direction of courtly romance.[3] While we may wish to retain the designation "heroic epic" when referring to the *Nibelungenlied,* it is with the awareness that it "has incorporated aspects of various worlds,"[4] and that this diversity is reflected, to some degree, in the style of the poet.

66

Nowhere is this more evident than in the author's choice of vocabulary and in certain syntactical structures. His debt to older forms is apparent in the use of such words as "degen, recke, helt, wîgant" (all of which can mean "hero" or "warrior"), "wine" ("spouse"), "verch" ("life"), "urliuge" ("war" or "battle"). Older adjectives retained in his text include "dürkel" ("riddled" with holes), "ellenhaft" ("manly"), "gremelîch" ("frightening," "awful"), "veige" ("marked for death"). Several older verbal forms are also attested, such as "dagen" ("to keep silent"), and "vreischen," ("to experience"). The poet's penchant for placing attributive adjectives after nouns is not always occasioned by metric considerations, but often by older tradition: "Albrich der vil starke" ("strong Albrich"), "Sîvrit der vil küene" ("brave Siegfried"). Frequently, archaic forms are employed in situations which contrast with a refined, courtly setting.

Many of the epithets used by the poet are "stock" items that occur with great frequency throughout the *Nibelungenlied,* as, for example, "stark" (with Siegfried), "rîch" (with Ute), "scoen" (with Kriemhild), "grimm" (with Hagen), and "guot" with Rüdeger. This also holds true for the first epithet used to describe Kriemhild in 2.1: "edel." In his commentary to this verse, de Boor remarks that the term was still used primarily as a designation of position within society, that is, to show that Kriemhild was of noble lineage. It is, however, also the last adjective used with Kriemhild in 2377.2: "ze stücken was gehouwen    dô daz edele wîp" ("The noble woman had been hacked to pieces"). The reader may wonder what the poet intended with "edel" in this context. Sympathy for Kriemhild and her plight? Irony? "Edel" is, after all, a thoroughly positive term. Even if understood simply as a designation of social status, the application of this epithet implies certain positive attributes on the part of the person with whom it is associated. Had the poet wished to indicate his own disgust with the level of degeneration reached by Kriemhild, he could have employed any number of pejoratives, including the trisyllabic "übele" ("wicked"), in greater accordance with the context. The contrast here between "ze stücken was gehouwen" and "daz edele wîp" seems to have been intentional. In a nostalgic sense, "edel" may recall memories of a time when Kriemhild was, in fact, the epitome of courtly breeding. But in its present context, the adjective has a decidedly ironic ring to it. Another instance in which an epithet is used with particular effect is in strophe 13, when the falcon of Kriemhild's dream is described as being "starc, scoen' und wilde" ("strong, handsome, and wild"). The first two adjectives are fairly common, but the choice of "wilde" gives the reader cause to reflect. "Starc" and "scoen' " allude to the external attributes of the lover Kriemhild is destined to meet. "Wilde" points to a more complex aspect of the "falcon's" nature. It is a word not normally associated with the more genteel world of the court. That which is designated as "wilde" can often stand in contrast and even opposition to courtly society. It may lack moderation, and may not feel bound to courtly mores. The word conveys to the reader the image of something, or someone, who belongs to another realm. It is an adjective which is frequently employed in Middle High German literature to designate the forest and ferocious animals, or in the form of a simile. (Note its particularly effective use in 976.3: "sam zwei wildiu pantel," "like two wild panthers.") The reader has thus been immediately alerted to the fact that the "falcon" which Kriemhild will rear is endowed with a trait that will set him apart from the rest of society. The use of adjectives in the *Nibelungenlied* is often somewhat rigid and formal, but in these two cases the epithets would appear to have been carefully selected for the given contexts, the first for its ironic dimension, the second for the specific message it may have conveyed to the medieval public.

The *Nibelungenlied* has often been compared with courtly romance[5] and, while one must remain conscious of the fact that it was written down at the highpoint of Arthurian idealism, its basic tenor sets it apart from its contemporaries. However, while some of its vocabulary reflects the spirit of an older, precourtly era, the language of chivalry is apparent in terms such as "harnasch" (from the Old French "harnas" and the Celtic "haiarn," "iron,") meaning "armor," "bûhurt" (Old French "bouhourt," signifying a courtly tournament involving the converging of two groups of knights), "puneiz" (Middle French "poingneis," Latin "pungere," with basically the same meaning as "bûhurt," although not confined to the tournament), "garzûn" (French "garçon," "page"). "Pirsen" or "birsen" (medieval Latin "bersa," "to stalk") reflects the influence of courtly language in the hunting sphere (note 916.2, where it is used ironically), while terms such as "palas" (French "palais," Latin "palatium," "palace"), "kolter" (Old French "coultre," Latin "culcitra," "blanket"), and "porte" (Latin "porta," "opening, gate") demonstrate the same influence in the domestic realm.

With respect to his choice of vocabulary, the *Nibelungenlied* poet stood between two worlds. While the closeness to courtly romance is evident in terms such as those cited above, as well as in more abstract concepts such as "tugent," "zuht," and "minneclîch," he tends to prefer concrete forms to abstractions.[6] Furthermore, the poet seems to adhere to more archaic forms when the content of his tale emanates from precourtly sources. In fact, he appears to have made a conscious effort on occasion to maintain, without necessarily striving to revitalize, older stylistic devices. Some, particularly formulaic constructions, may simply have been taken over from what was originally an oral means of transmission. The author had no reason to purge his text of such forms; they frequently suited his purpose admirably, contributing to the more primitive, precourtly atmosphere which prevails in many sections of the poem.[7] What is striking about this master is his adeptness at describing, in detail, life at the court, with its festivals, tournaments, knighting ceremonies, splendid attire, and beautiful women, as well as his talent for depicting graphically mass battle scenes, the comportment of heroes facing extinction, and confrontations between leading figures. Regardless of the milieu, "the author of the Nibelungenlied understood how to impart the dynamic content in a manner which was both linguistically and stylistically appropriate."[8]

Limitations of space prohibit a detailed discussion of the entire scope of rhetorical devices to be found in the *Nibelungenlied*.[9] Moreover, we cannot always be sure when such devices are used intentionally by the poet, thus implying special significance within a given context. Several figures of speech, such as irony, hyperbole, and simile, stand out, however, and will be treated briefly in the following pages.

I have already alluded to the irony associated with the use of "edel" to describe Kriemhild in 2377.2. The same might also be said for the application of "snell" to depict Gunther as he hangs from a nail on the wall where he has been put by Brünhild following his unsuccessful attempt to make love to her: " 'Ouch het ichs wênic êre,' sprach der snelle man" (" 'I, too, would gain little honor by it,' the brave man said," 641.1). The word "snell" has a number of meanings, all of them positive, including "adroit" and "mighty," adding yet a further ironic touch to its use in this instance. Furthermore, the word "grimm" describing Gunther's disposition in 142.4 does not accord with the king's performance throughout the

greater part of the *Nibelungenlied*. While it is an adjective well suited
for Hagen, it seems singularly inappropriate for Gunther. Although
Panzer has pointed out that the formulaic application of adjectives
in the *Nibelungenlied* can tend to rob some of the figures of their
individuality, [10] the poet uses his epithets as ironic barbs with great
efficacy. His characterization of the timid Huns in 1792.4 as "die
übermüeten degene" ("these proud warriors") gives the reader cause
to smile, [11] and nothing can better attest to his sense of irony than
the use of "minneclîch" ("lovely," "charming," "delightful") to
designate Brünhild in 425.4:

> "Den stein sol er werfen    unt springen dar nâch,
> den gêr mit mir schiezen;    lât iu sîn niht ze gâch.
> ir muget wol hie verliesen    die êre und ouch den lîp.
> des bedenket iuch vil ebene,"    sprach daz minneclîche wîp.

("He must throw the boulder and leap over it, and he must also compete
against me in the javelin throw. Don't be in too great a hurry to try it.
You could well lose both your honor and your life here. Think it over
very carefully," said the charming woman.)

It is not only in his choice of epithets that the poet demonstrates
his ironic technique. Irony is a trait which is most appropriately
associated with Hagen, and nowhere is this more apparent than in
the fifteenth *Aventiure* when he attempts to get Kriemhild to divulge
Siegfried's one vulnerable spot. In reference to the bad blood prevailing between Brünhild and Kriemhild, Hagen remarks: " 'ir wert
versüenet    wol nâch disen tagen' " (" 'The two of you will certainly
be reconciled within the next few days,' " 895.1). Knowing full
well what Hagen intends, the reader must gauge him at this point
to be a ruthless, scheming, even demonic figure, who can refer to
the woman he must despise as "vil liebiu vrouwe mîn" ("my dear
lady," 905.1).

Symptomatic of a conscious heroic-archaic stylization is the poet's
use of hyperbole. This is especially evident in the manner in which
he deals with scenes involving blood. When Kriemhild discovers
that it is the body of Siegfried which has been placed before her
chamber, the incredible grief which she perceives causes the blood
to spurt from her mouth: "daz bluot ir ûz dem munde    von herzen
jâmer brast" (1010.2), and when she looks upon Siegfried for the

last time, blood instead of tears flows from her bright eyes: "diu ir vil liehten ougen    vor leide weineten bluot" (1069.4). During a lull in the battle between Burgundians and Huns in the thirty-fifth *Aventiure*, the blood can be seen flowing through holes in the walls of Attila's Great Hall: "daz bluot allenthalben    durch diu löcher vlôz" (2078.2).

The poet displays a penchant for using large numbers, particularly multiples of 1,000. When Siegfried offers his assistance to Gunther in the campaign against the Saxons and the Danes, he asks the Burgundian king for 1,000 men (161), even though the enemy numbers over 40,000 (170.2). During the trip to Gran, Hagen ferries over ten thousand knights and pages across the Danube. Later, the Burgundians throw 7,000 dead Huns as well as scores of wounded from the Great Hall (2013). This tendency to work with large numbers accords well with the poet's intention to emphasize the full extent of the calamity at the conclusion of the *Nibelungenlied*. Through their application in the latter *Aventiuren*, the transition from personal to collective tragedy is underscored in a most effective manner, allowing the reader to acquire a sense of mass annihilation, of the demise of entire peoples.

In his use of metaphor, the poet was deliberately sparing, perhaps because of his preference for direct expression. The most striking example might be drawn from the thirty-eighth *Aventiure*, when Dietrich's men, the Amelungs, "holten ûz den helmen    den heize vliezenden bach" ("drew that hot flowing stream from their [the Burgundians'] helmets," 2288.4). By contrast, the application of simile is more extensive. Kriemhild is referred to as one who appears "alsô der morgenrôt / tuot ûz den trüeben wolken" ("like the red morning sun from behind the dark clouds," 281.1b–2a). Two strophes later, she is compared to "der liehte mâne" ("the bright moon," 283.1). The same cosmic simile is applied to Siegfried by Kriemhild: "wie rehte hêrlîche    er vor den recken gât, / alsam der liehte mâne    vor den sternen tuot" ("How magnificently he excels before the other knights, just as the bright moon outshines the stars," 817.2–3). In the first instance, the comparison is made by the narrator and underscores Kriemhild's splendor. It is uncomplicated with respect to the effect intended upon the reader or listener. Kriemhild's beauty is unique, even worthy of cosmic association. But her own likening of Siegfried to the moon is not so innocent. It represents a social faux pas in the presence of Brünhild, and it is

also an indication of her *superbia,* since she is quite aware, as the
ensuing argument demonstrates, of what it signifies to be married
to the only man worthy of comparison, in her eyes, to a primary
celestial body.

Particularly noteworthy is the poet's penchant for similes involving wild animals. In 97.2, the dwarf Albrich and Siegfried are
compared by Hagen to "die lewen wilde" ("wild lions"), and Gunther
and Siegfried are described as "zwei wildiu pantel" ("two wild panthers") in 976.3. As Dancwart wreaks havoc among the Huns, he
is compared to an "eberswîn" ("wild boar," 1946.3), as is Volker
in 2001.3. Timm has remarked that similes in the *Nibelungenlied*
are not used simply as artistic devices aimed at making the text
more pleasing from an aesthetic point of view, but that they are
employed at decisive moments in the text.[12] Both sets of similes
discussed here would appear to substantiate his theory.

In their commentary to 976.2–3, the race to the drinking well,
Mowatt and Sacker state: "Is perhaps the whole hunt scene a homosexual hunt, with Hagen and Sifrid the two wild boars of Kriemhilde's dream (921.2), and fatal penetration from the rear Sifrid's
punishment for not caring about Worms?"[13] Symbolism gone awry,
the reader may query and, in this instance, rightly so. Does Siegfried's death "symbolize" anything or is it simply a depiction of the
murder of the hero by a treacherous Hagen? In strophe 1002 we
read:

> Do erbiten si der nahte    und fuoren über Rîn.
> von helden kunde nimmer    wirs gejaget sîn.
> ein tier, daz si sluogen,    daz weinten edliu kint.
> jâ muosen sîn engelten    vil guote wîgande sint.

(They waited until nightfall and went back across the Rhine. Warriors
could never have participated in a worse hunt. The quarry which they
slew was lamented by noble maidens and many good warriors were later
to pay for his death.)

It is quite appropriate to speak of "hunt symbolism" in the
sixteenth and seventeeth *Aventiuren,* with Siegfried, "ein tier," the
hunted, and Hagen the hunter. However, to consider his death as
representative of the death of a sun god as advocates of the mythical
approach have been inclined to do, or as symbolic of a "fatal"

homosexual relationship, is imprudent. The poet seems to have been content in portraying the hunter as the hunted. Whether he or his public viewed the episode as signifying anything else is impossible to determine.

The question of symbolism within the *Nibelungenlied* is a complicated one and a matter which the reader and critic must approach with extreme care. The falcon of Kriemhild's first dream is clearly symbolic of her first husband, as she is later informed by Ute, and the two eagles represent Hagen and Gunther, as do the wild boars of strophe 921 and the two mountains of 924. When Ute dreams that all the birds of the land are dead (1509.4), it is clear from the context that this can be taken as a reference to the Burgundian warriors. When Hagen destroys the boat in which he has ferried the knights and pages across the Danube (1581), he offers the rational explanation that this will prevent any coward from turning back. But in view of what Hagen has learned from the water sprite, it may be interpreted as a symbolic act, signifying the entry into another world from which no one of the party is to return. As such, it may also be viewed as an indication of Hagen's acceptance of fate.

There are other instances, however, when the ultimate meaning of an act or a particular description is not so apparent. It is not difficult to see "symbolic" significance where such may have been quite unintended by the poet.[14] When Siegfried lies fatally wounded among the flowers, the narrator comments: "Dô viel in die bluo-men    der Kriemhilde man. / daz bluot von sîner wunden    sach man vil vâste gan" ("Kriemhild's husband then fell among the flowers. One could see the blood flowing from his wound," 988.1–2). Timm recognized here a contrast between the flowing blood and the blossoming flowers, and contended that the "individuality" of the motif—used only with the dying Siegfried—underscored its older, mythological significance, and that the flowers symbolized the hope for a new life.[15] Such a symbolic interpretation of this scene is unwarranted, however, as it fails to take into account the final outcome of the epic with its basically nihilistic tenor. The role accorded nature in the *Nibelungenlied* is a modest one, and there is no evidence to support the hypothesis that the poet intended Siegfried's death among the flowers to symbolize the "great chain of being," the perpetual cycle of life and death. The image is not one in which both the dying and the living are accorded equal significance. The accent is clearly on the former.[16]

Before turning our attention to the structure of the *Nibelungenlied*, it is fitting to comment briefly on the author's use of a narrator and the function of dialogues within the work. A large portion of the epic is related by a fictitious narrator, never identified, and only with great care and reservation to be associated with the poet himself. The narrator opens and closes the *Nibelungenlied*, indicating from the outset that his public will "hear" tales of admirable knights, of battle and misfortune, and concluding with a reference to "iu" ("you," 2379.1) that he cannot say what occurred after the slaughter at Gran except that lamentation on a massive scale was the lot of those who survived the carnage. In 8.1b, in a half-verse of little consequence, the narrator appears as a person, utilizing the first-person singular: "Die drîe künege wâren, als ich gesaget hân" ("The three kings were, as I have stated . . . "). In 10.4b, he testifies to his inability to name all of the Burgundian knights. In both cases, the interjection by the narrator is of little consequence. On occasion, he may seek to establish a bond with his public as in 583.3b, when he maintains that "we" may certainly state that never had so many women assembled for a reception: "(des wir wol mügen jehen)." Within the same context, the narrator allows himself a judgmental "aside" regarding the obligation of the knights to participate in the jousting (584.2b).

Hansjürgen Linke has pointed to the manner in which the narrator "unites" with his public in 778.1 (suggesting that they now turn their attention away from the Burgundians, who are preparing for the festival), 1506.1 (similar to 778.1 in function), and 1655.1 (where he also suggests that it is time to turn from one thing to another).[17] But the narrator's comments are not always so bland. While he may be slow to castigate and relatively quick to praise (note 152.3b, 1398.2b, 1599.4b, 1722.1b),[18] his use of the epithet "ungetriuwen" ("treacherous") in 988.4 leaves no doubt as to where his sentiments lie in the matter of Siegfried's murder. Yet he, too, has nothing pejorative to say of Hagen in the latter stages of the work (apart from the allusion to "übermuot" in 1865.4 which is, however, applicable to all of the Burgundians). For the narrator, as well as for Dietrich, Hildebrand, Rüdeger et al., time appears to have relativized the crime committed in the sixteenth *Aventiure*.

While on occasion he may allow himself a personal judgment of either a positive or a negative nature, the narrator remains, on the whole, remarkably neutral with respect to a more encompassing statement on the final outcome of the confrontation between Burgundians and Huns. He makes no attempt to persuade his public, at least directly, to condemn, or condone, their actions. As is the case with his reader, he senses the presence of another element, a demonic force which motivates Kriemhild to conspire against her kin and bring the world to its knees: "Ich waene der übel vâlant Kriemhilde daz geriet, / daz sie sich mit friuntschefte von *Gunthere* schiet" ("I believe the wicked devil advised Kriemhild to break her pact of friendship with Gunther," 1394. 1–2). [19] When all order disintegrates at the conclusion of the work, the narrator, in final union with his public, also stands aghast, but unwilling, or unable, to offer any final judgment.

Over one third of the *Nibelungenlied,* according to Panzer, [20] consists of dialogues that may be considered the "dramatic highlights" of the epic. It is through scenes involving dialogues that the reader gains insight into the motivations and characters of the major figures: the arrogance of Siegfried and the pathetic helplessness of Gunther in the third *Aventiure,* the egocentricity of Kriemhild and the (justifiably) suspicious nature of Brünhild in the fourteenth, Hagen's deceitfulness and Kriemhild's naiveté in the fifteenth, and, in particular, Kriemhild's depravity in contrast to the exemplary comportment of her antagonist in the thirty-ninth. It may well have been such episodes which caused Hebbel to remark on the poet's great talent as a dramatist (see below, chapter 5). Through dialogue, the characters come to life as no others in medieval German literature, and their strengths, weaknesses, and passions are laid bare. In the final confrontation between Hagen and Kriemhild, the Burgundian hero, while defeated in battle, demonstrates, through the last words he will ever utter, that he has, in fact, proved himself to be Kriemhild's superior, that the inner victory is his: "den schaz den weiz nu niemen wan got unde mîn: / der sol dich, vâlandinne, immer wol verholn sîn" ("Now no one knows, other than God and I, where the treasure is hidden. It shall always remain hidden from you, you devil," 2371.3–4). It is not only a highpoint in the *Nibelungenlied,* but also of Hagen's existence. His words demonstrate that he is, despite his outer misfortune, a sovereign being. At the same time, they are, of course, terrible evidence of the fact that his life concludes on a basically egocentric note, for while he may "triumph" over Kriemhild, he has helped to bring about the demise of the clan he had sworn to serve and protect.

## Structure

From the beginning of the epic, allusions to pending misfortune help to mold the work into a unified whole. In contrast to courtly romance, where such predictions are rare, the use of allusions in the *Nibelungenlied* represents a salient feature of the poet's style. Siegfried Beyschlag has demonstrated that they are also an important structural component within the poem.[21] Usually contained within the final verse of a strophe, these (normally ominous) allusions often constitute a striking contrast to the prevailing atmosphere of festivity and harmony evident on the surface and, as such, underscore the dichotomy between reality and appearance which runs throughout the *Nibelungenlied.* They serve as a constant reminder to the reader that a catastrophe is in the making. Friedrich Panzer has compared their function to that of the classical chorus, accompanying the action and issuing warnings.[22] There are no great surprises to be expected,[23] but, through his use of allusion, the poet succeeds in heightening the suspense from the outset. His public is inspired to read on (or continue listening, as the case may be), to determine how events leading up to this tragedy will unfold.

Nine *Aventiuren* close with an ominous prediction (1, 3, 5, 14, 18, 24, 28, 30, 31),[24] and portents of disaster abound within the individual *Aventiuren.* Already in the first, there are no fewer than five major references to future strife. Two of the more poignant are contained in 2.4 and 6.4: "dar umbe muosen degene     vil verliesen den lîp" ("For this reason many warriors were to lose their lives"); "si sturben sît jaemerlîche     von zweier edelen frouwen nît" ("They later were to die a miserable death as a result of the jealousy of two noble women"). By the time one reaches the concluding strophe of the first *Aventiure,* the integral aspects of the plot have been presented in the form of allusions or dreams: "wie sêre si daz rach / an ir naehsten mâgen,     die in sluogen sint! / durch sîn eines sterben starp vil maneger muoter kint" ("How terribly she avenged that [that is, Siegfried's murder] on her next-of-kin who had killed him! Many a mother's child was to die as a result of his death," 19.2b–4). A portent of total catastrophe such as this is calculated not only to increase tension and enhance interest. Together with similar allusions, it helps to establish the unity between the two major sections of the *Nibelungenlied.* As such, these predictions comprise a structural device of great significance, demonstrating very early that there is an inherent connection between the death of an individual and subsequent mass slaughter, that there is to be an eventual escalation from personal to collective tragedy.

While it is not possible here to examine all of the allusions to impending catastrophe, a few remarks on the prolific employment of this device in the twenty-fifth *Aventiure* seem appropriate. The eighty strophes which comprise this *Aventiure* deal with the journey of the Burgundians to the point where they are ferried across the Danube by Hagen. In 1507.4, reference is made, by the narrator, to the sorrow later perceived by those who remain at home: "die si dâ heime liezen,    die beweinetenz sît" (Those whom they left at home were later to lament their departure"). In the following strophe, an old bishop remarks to Ute: "got müez' ir êre dâ bewarn" ("May God protect their lives there" 1508.4b), and in 1513.4, a specific reference is made to Hagen's subsequent feats in battle against the Huns: "sît wart von im verhouwen    vil manic helm unde rant" ("Later, many a helmet and shield rim would be hacked to pieces by him"). Both narrator and characters see the danger emanating from Kriemhild (note 1516.4, 1517.4, and 1518.4). The theme of *leit* is repeated in 1520.4, 1521.4, and 1523.3. At no time in the *Nibelungenlied* are the portents of catastrophe so concentrated as in this *Aventiure,* where they culminate in the chilling prediction of the water sprite that all who ride to Attila's court are doomed (1540). They are instrumental in creating an image of the Burgundians as a group already associated with the realm of the dead, and it is no coincidence that they occur so frequently at a point when the party, with Hagen's assistance, effects a literal transfer across the swollen Danube into another world from which there is no return.

Complementing such references is the poet's use of the dream as *praemonitio.* Kriemhild's falcon dream in the first *Aventiure,* as well as those she relates to Siegfried in the sixteenth, allude to the demise of her husband. They are, however, limited in scope. Kriemhild's dreams are visions of a personal tragedy and, although they are clearly intended as warnings, they are either not acted upon or their significance is completely underestimated. The same is true of Ute's dream in the twenty-fifth *Aventiure* when she envisions the death of all the birds of the land (1509). The symbolism of Kriemhild's original dream (bird = warrior) has been retained, if in slightly modified form, but the individual has now been replaced by the collective.

These and other predictions of dire misfortune are a stock device of the *Nibelungenlied* poet, and he uses them with great effectiveness to create an atmosphere of impending disaster. Regardless of the superficial harmony which may still prevail on occasion (for example, at Bechelaren), the reader is constantly reminded of how things are to turn out, and has been given the impression that, from the outset, fate is irrevocable.[25]

Tension is also increased by the occasional use of *spannende Pausen* ("retarding moments"). The argument between Kriemhild and Brünhild in the fourteenth *Aventiure,* for example, is "interrupted," or, rather, presented in stages for heightened effect. The first segment transpires as the women observe the tournament (814–30); there follows a pause of seven strophes during which Kriemhild and her ladies-in-waiting prepare themselves for mass and proceed to the minster. In the following five strophes (838–42), the argument is continued in a much more heated fashion, and Kriemhild hurls her ultimate insult at Brünhild. But there follows yet another interruption of three strophes devoted to the actual mass, subsequent to which the confrontation continues, this time with Kriemhild presenting the "proof" of her accusation. The same technique is used by the poet to even greater effect in the second part of the epic, particularly after the Burgundians have arrived at Gran. Although Gunther and his men appear in Attila's camp in the twenty-eighth *Aventiure,* the massacre of the Burgundian pages by Hunnish forces under Bloedel does not take place until the thirty-second *Aventiure,* and the initial fighting in the Great Hall breaks out in the thirty-third. Kriemhild and Hagen confront each other on several occasions before hostilities break out on a grand scale, and Volker's slaying of a garish Hun in the thirty-first *Aventiure* threatens to bring matters to a head. But in every instance the final reckoning is postponed. The reader knows, of course, that a massive confrontation is inevitable. The paramount question is: when will the point be reached when words are followed by action? To some degree, these "retarding moments" may also create the vain hope that the inevitable can somehow be circumvented.

On occasion, the reader encounters parenthetical interjections which do not seem to benefit the text and which can, in fact, interrupt the smooth flow of the action. Two such superfluous comments appear in 107.2b and 107.3b:

"Mir wart gesaget maere    in mînes vater lant,
daz hie bî iu waeren    (daz het ich gern' erkant)
die küenesten recken    (des hân ich vil vernomen)
die ie künec gewunne;    dar umbe bin ich her bekomen."

("I have been told in my father's land that here at your court [I'd like to see if this is the case] are to be found the bravest knights who ever served a king [I certainly took note of that]. That's why I've come here.")

Neither 2b nor 3b add anything significant in terms of content. In fact, read together, verses 1, 2a, 3a, and 4 are quite comprehensible. 2b and 3b were necessary for metrical reasons, but, when read in context, they create an awkward impression. Such interjections, whether by the narrator or a character, are simply "fillers," and are generally of little consequence from a semantic perspective.

In the preceding pages, we have been concerned with structural devices employed by the poet. A more comprehensive structural analysis of the *Nibelungenlied* cannot be undertaken without the realization that, as Helmut de Boor has stated, there exists today less of a consensus in the matter of the poem's structure than ever before.[26] Numerous attempts have been made to discern a symmetrical construction within the epic, but the variety of hypotheses is such as to exclude any definitive scheme which might be considered intentional on the part of the poet.[27] It has been suggested that the *Nibelungenlied* can be divided into three sections, with the first nineteen *Aventiuren* comprising "Siegfried's Death," the twentieth *Aventiure* constituting a "bridge" between the first and the second half, and *Aventiuren* 21 to 39 forming the section which deals with "Kriemhild's Revenge" and the demise of the Burgundians. This strikes me as a very convenient, but somewhat arbitrary, effort to arrive at the symmetrical structure 19–1–19. Thematically, there is no reason to separate the twentieth *Aventiure* from the second "half" of the work. It is concerned with the conditions prevailing in Hungary following the death of Queen Helche, and the decision taken by Attila to woo Kriemhild. The twentieth *Aventiure* is, in fact, an integral part of the second section of the work, and includes such an important element as the oath sworn by Rüdeger to avenge any wrong done Kriemhild. Moreover, a new geographical focus is provided, and Gran, Attila's court, is established as a potential counterpole to Worms. Put simply, then, manuscript B of the

*Nibelungenlied* can be divided into two parts, with the first nineteen *Aventiuren* (strophes 1–1142) owing much to the older Siegfried tradition, while the following twenty (strophes 1143–2379) revolve around the downfall of the Burgundians and Huns.

Both Helmut de Boor and Burghart Wachinger have emphasized the tendency of the *Nibelungenlied* poet to present his tale in blocks of strophes or *Aventiuren*.[28] For de Boor, four larger blocks are discernible, two in each section of the epic: the first begins with Siegfried's participation in the war against the Saxons and Danes in the fourth *Aventiure* and concludes with his return to Xanten. The second encompasses the invitation to visit Worms and culminates in Siegfried's murder and the period spent by Kriemhild mourning his death in Worms. In the second section of the poem, the first larger block is introduced by Attila's suit for Kriemhild's hand and closes with the ascension of the grieving widow to the position of queen of the Huns. The final block in the *Nibelungenlied* concludes with the slaughter of Burgundians and Huns and Kriemhild's death.

This division of the epic in accordance with larger "plot units" is not only convincing, it avoids the problems so often encountered with efforts to demonstrate numerical symmetry, namely, that the interpreter must deal somewhat arbitrarily with particular strophes, and even *Aventiuren,* in order to arrive at a neat structure. Furthermore, within the blocks concerned, certain parallel structures may be ascertained to which we shall now turn our attention.

Both sections of the *Nibelungenlied* involve wooing missions and marriages with radical consequences. Parallel to Siegfried's wooing of Kriemhild is Attila's offer of marriage to the queen in the twentieth *Aventiure*. As in the first part of the epic, Kriemhild departs Worms; she lives in relative peace until her relatives arrive in Gran. At this point, serious problems arise which blood ties can do nothing to mitigate. It is quite apparent that we are dealing here primarily with the consequences of Kriemhild's marriages. In the first instance, she becomes the spouse of an individual who, through his very existence, represents a perpetual threat to Worms and Burgundian power. Kriemhild herself is not deliberately and consciously opposed to her brothers as Siegfried's wife, but her awareness and appreciation of the power and status acquired through her union with the hero of Xanten place her squarely on his side. In the second part of the *Nibelungenlied,* however, Gran is established as a hostile counterpart to Worms as soon as Kriemhild becomes queen of the

Huns. Her marriage to Attila, one of convenience, and agreed upon by Kriemhild with only one thing in mind, namely, to achieve revenge for her murdered Siegfried, is a prelude to catastrophe on a grand scale, as her marriage to Siegfried had been on an individual level.

In both sections of the *Nibelungenlied*, a similar thematic structure is evident: a hero appears at Worms, either in person (Siegfried) or represented by a liegeman (Attila-Rüdeger), woos Kriemhild, and, as a consequence of the subsequent union, comes into conflict with the Burgundians. Death is the ultimate result. There is a period following Siegfried's return to Xanten with Kriemhild which could create the impression that the work will end on a happy note, just as in the second part of the epic, the time following Kriemhild's marriage to Attila is basically one of superficial tranquillity and harmony. It is the "calm before the storm." As in the first part of the *Nibelungenlied*, it is the "reuniting" of Kriemhild and the Burgundians after the queen has been removed for some time from her family's sphere of influence, which leads directly to strife and turmoil. It could be said that the entire epic is structured around Kriemhild: "The unity of the work lies in the unity of the plot and the major figures. At the center of the plot is Kriemhild."[29] With Kriemhild as the focal point of a unified *Nibelungenlied*, the structure of the epic may be illustrated in a schematic manner as follows:

Part One

1. Kriemhild's self-imposed exile in Worms due to her fear of *leit* caused by love.

2. Marriage to Siegfried and removal from Worms. Integration into Siegfried's world which is a threat to Burgundian power.

    Kriemhild already in conflict with Worms before departure for Xanten. (Demand that Hagen and Ortwin accompany her.)

    Pause

3. New meeting with Burgundians. Kriemhild aware of her considerable power and stature. Intensified conflict as a result of Kriemhild's ruthlessness. *Superbia.* Insensitive toward family.

4. Catastrophe: Death of Siegfried.

    *Leit* paramount.

Part Two

1. Kriemhild's self-imposed exile in Worms as a result of inflicted *leit*.

2. Marriage to Attila and removal from Worms. Integration into Attila's world which she turns into a threat to Burgundy.

   Kriemhild in conflict with Worms before and after her departure for Gran.

                                      Pause

3. New meeting with Burgundians. Kriemhild prepared to use power to avenge Siegfried. Various confrontations with Hagen. *Superbia*. Kriemhild ruthless and insensitive toward all.

4. Catastrophe: Death of Kriemhild and decimation of Huns and Burgundians.

   *Leit* paramount.

What is apparent from this structure is the primary significance of Kriemhild for the work as a whole as well as the importance of the concept of *leit* from a thematic perspective.[30] The allusions to future sorrow are manifold in the initial strophes of the *Nibelungenlied* and are consistently linked to the person of Kriemhild. In essence, the concept of *leit* forms a framework for the unravelling of the plot and simultaneously reflects the basically nihilistic attitude of the narrator (and perhaps also of the poet). This brief structural analysis also demonstrates the manner in which Kriemhild becomes increasingly divorced from her family and the court at Worms, and that her marriages to two of the most powerful men in the world run counter to the basic interests of her clan.

It would be imprudent to claim that the *Nibelungenlied* poet exhibited "exemplary style," that there are no "inconsistencies, obscurities, or prevarications"[31] in the poem, or that the "intended" structure of the epic is as apparent to the modern reader as it may have been to the author's public at the turn of the thirteenth century. It is not a flawless work of art. What may be regarded as "shortcomings" today were, however, quite possibly viewed as "strong points" at the time the epic was written down or recited. If repetitive formulaic constructions, for example, tend to run counter to a modern reader's aesthetic sense, they were undoubtedly integral to the oral presentation of the tale and there is no reason to believe that they necessarily caused any consternation on the part of the medieval public when they were retained in the written version. What is remarkable is that the *Nibelungenlied,* despite what we may consider to be its "weaknesses" today, continues to generate such enthusiasm and a sense of awe, almost 800 years after it was committed to parchment. Such ebullience emanates primarily from the fascination with the inner dynamic of the poem. The *Nibelungenlied* is a unified work of art and its integrality is realized through a successful combination of inner substance and outer form which justifies its designation as the most impressive literary monument from the German High Middle Ages.

## Chapter Five

# The Reception of the *Nibelungenlied* in Germany from the *Klage* to the Twentieth Century

If the number of popular and artistic works based on the *Nibelungenlied* may be considered evidence of the attraction the epic held for subsequent generations of readers and theatergoers, then we may certainly conclude that the poem has proved to be one of the most inspiring "sources" in the history of German literature. I have already considered in the Introduction the extent to which the *Nibelungenlied* has captured scholarly interest from the time of Obereit and Bodmer to the present. But what of the influence the work exerted in the literary sphere subsequent to its genesis in the form known to us from the turn of the thirteenth century? Actually, it is more appropriate to speak of the influence of the *Nibelungen* tradition per se, although this is not meant to diminish the significance of the *Nibelungenlied* for the later creative process. The scores of dramas written during the nineteenth and twentieth centuries, for example, are almost entirely based on the epic. However, the popular *Lied vom Hürnen Seyfrid* (The lay of Seyfrid, the Dragon-Slayer) together with its analogues, the play by Hans Sachs and the folk book, is more indebted to the Nordic sources which relate *in extenso* of Siegfried's youth. The same is true of Wagner's *Ring des Nibelungen, (Ring of the Nibelungen)* the mythological elements of which hark back to the *Edda* and the *Völsunga Saga*. The *Nibelungenlied* is part of a remarkably rich tradition which spans centuries in terms of its literary expression.

Within the framework of the present monograph, it is impossible to provide more than a basic overview of the subsequent literary treatment of the *Nibelungen* tradition and the *Nibelungenlied* itself. For the most part, I have not considered the nonliterary manifestations of the subject matter (film, postcards, art, etc.). The number of dramas, poems, and novels based on the *Nibelungenlied* alone is legion, and while I have felt it appropriate to linger for a while in some instances and offer the reader a more intimate glimpse of the intentions of a particular author (thereby exposing my own prejudices), I have made no attempt to treat systematically every literary work which uses the epic as a base. For the reception of the *Nibelungenlied* in Germany during the nineteenth and twentieth centuries, I have to acknowledge a heavy debt to the studies of Holger Schulz,[1] Otfrid Ehrismann,[2] and Werner Wunderlich,[3] works which may accurately be designated as indispensable for anyone who wishes to gain insight into the great proclivity of *Nibelungen* materials produced over the past two hundred years.

## Diu Klage

*Diu Klage* (The lament) is "a brief inferior sequel"[4] to the *Nibelungenlied,* an elegiac commentary of 4,360 verses in rhyming couplets, appended to all of the major manuscripts of its great predecessor.[5] The *Klage* is, at one and the same time, a commentary on events which transpire in the *Nibelungenlied,* a defense of Kriemhild as well as a condemnation of Hagen, and a narration of the course of events subsequent to the mass slaughter in the Great Hall of Attila. Above all, it is an elegy addressed to the prominent figures who are no more, as well as to the masses of Burgundians and Huns slain during the fray.

On the question of Siegfried's "guilt," the anonymous poet is unambiguous in assigning the hero a share of the responsibility for bringing about his death: "unt daz er selbe den tôt / gewan von sîner übermuot" ("Until he himself was killed as a result of his haughtiness," 38–39). No details of the actual murder are provided, although the blame for the deed is placed on Gunther (103), Hagen (104), and Brünhild (104) respectively. The poet also emphasizes the excessive lamenting of Kriemhild (95–96), but, unlike the author of the *Nibelungenlied,* who is inclined to consider such a lack of moderation as unnatural and destructive, and who, at least in manuscript B, paints a most uncomplimentary picture of the queen as a she-devil, the *Klage* poet takes Kriemhild's side and praises her actions. No one, he asserts, should condemn her for wishing to avenge Siegfried's death (139), a less than veiled criticism, perhaps,

of those before him who have portrayed Kriemhild from a decidedly
negative point of view. His response to such criticism is summed
up in verses 154–58:

> swer ditze maere merken kan,
> der sagt unschuldic gar ir lîp,
> wan daz daz vil edel werde wîp
> taete nâch ir triuwe
> ir râche in grôzer riuwe.

(Whoever can take note of this tale will declare that the queen was guiltless.
For the noble lady acted out of loyalty, exacting her revenge in great
sorrow.)

It is, in fact, her loyalty which, the poet proclaims, will assure
her a place in heaven (571–76). Earlier, however, when considering
the loss of forty thousand men prior to the death of Hagen (236–
37), the author had explicitly stated that Kriemhild's decision to
let matters run their course had emanated "von krankem sinne"
("from a sick mind," 243), which hardly seems to accord with his
later defense of the queen. Moreover, to associate Kriemhild's loyalty
and the deeds she has committed as a result of it with her right to
a place in Heaven gives us cause to wonder if the poet was aware
of the basic tenets of Christianity. He (or she?) was caught between
justifying Kriemhild's quest for revenge on the one hand, and the
horror perceived at the extent of the catastrophe on the other. Hildebrand's killing of Kriemhild is condemned (732–33). Hildebrand
had hewn Kriemhild to pieces because she had cut down a defenseless
Hagen. In the *Klage*, however, Hildebrand soundly condemns the
late Hagen for all that has transpired, according him, in fact, the
appellation *vâlant* so poignantly used to depict a demonic Kriemhild
in the *Nibelungenlied* (note *Klage*, 1250). The Burgundians, as a
whole, allowed their *übermuot* to prevent them from telling Attila
about the true state of affairs at a time when the monarch might
well have taken measures to circumvent the mass slaughter which
later ensued (284–89). Hildebrand also refers to this *übermuot* in
1277 and sees it as the reason for the fact that the Burgundians
have been afflicted by "den gotes slac" ("God's wrath," 1276).

The *Klage* utilizes four major geographical locations: Attila's court,
Bechelaren, Passau, and Worms. Rüdeger, the "vater aller tugende"

("epitome of virtue," 2133), is particularly mourned, the poet claiming that "an dem was mit wârheit / verlorn der werlde wünne" ("With him was lost, in truth, the joy of the world," 1962–63). In Passau, Bishop Pilgrim puts the blame for all that has happened exclusively on Hagen, maintaining that one should rue the day that he was born (3420). In Worms, Rumold refers to "Hagenen übermuot" (4031) as well as to his "grôzen untriuwen" ("great treachery," 4035). The intention is clear: the poet is attempting to absolve Kriemhild as much as possible of guilt for the catastrophe, and Hagen, a totally dark figure, is to bear the blame, or at least the major part of it. There are frequent references to the wrath of God, and in general we may say that Christian overtones (as confused as they may be) are more conspicuous in the *Klage* than in the *Nibelungenlied*.[6] In an attempt to provide a more optimistic outlook on the future, the poet refers to the impending coronation of young Siegfried, Brünhild's son, in Worms. The land cannot remain without a king, and both Brünhild and the surviving Burgundian nobility find consolation in the forthcoming ceremony.

As a defense of Kriemhild and a condemnation of Hagen, the *Klage* leaves us unconvinced. The black and white attitude of the poet in no way accords with the text of the *Nibelungenlied* or the intention of its author. The author lacked the depth and perspective of his forerunner and clearly had little sympathy with the ambivalent disposition of the latter toward his main characters. The weak attempt to provide some sort of happy ending to the tragedy stands in blatant contrast to the conclusion of the *Nibelungenlied*. The final section of the *Klage* (4323–60) adds some (probably unintentional) levity to the predominant atmosphere of despair, as the poet expresses his regret at not being able to inform us of the fate of Attila, whether he was taken up into the air, buried alive, brought to Heaven, whether he climbed out of his skin, scurried away into a hole in the wall, or went to hell and was consumed by the devil.

## Late Medieval and Early Baroque Renditions of the Young Siegfried Story

Working from ten of eleven extant prints of the *Lied vom Hürnen Seyfrid (The lay of Seyfrid, the Dragon-Slayer)*, K. C. King published, in 1958, a critical edition of this early New High German poem, dating from the late fifteenth century.[7] The work consists of 179

eight-line stanzas with the rhyme scheme A B C B D E F E. The
*Lied* harks back to a source with which the *Nibelungenlied* poet was
probably familiar, but which he did not exploit to full advantage.
It is primarily concerned with Seyfrid's (Siegfried's) adventures as a
young man, his fight with a dragon, his almost total invulnerability
acquired by bathing in the slain dragon's blood, and his love of
Kriemhild, daughter of King Gybich. Seyfrid subsequently rescues
the princess from the lair of a dragon and undergoes a series of
adventures culminating in his slaying of the giant Kuperan with
the aid of a dwarf. The poem closes with a reference to the growing
jealousy of Hagen and Gyrnot, and the later death of Seyfrid at the
hands of Hagen.

Noteworthy in the *Lied* is the fact that, from the outset, Seyfrid
is portrayed as a brash young man who is self-assertive and physically
strong, but not given to listening to others:

> Der knab was so můtwillig
> Darzů starck und auch gross
> Das seyn vatter und můter
> Der ding gar seer verdross
> Er wolt nie keynem menschen
> Seyn tag seyn underthon
> Im stund seyn syn und můte
> Das er nur zůg daruon.
>
> (Stanza 2)

(The boy was strong and tall but also so headstrong that his father and
mother became quite concerned about him. He never wanted to be subordinated to anyone, and all he could ever think of was getting away.)

The tendency to assert himself and to ignore the status of others
is reflected in stanzas 173 through 176, as Seyfrid arouses animosity
in King Gunther and his brothers, leading to his subsequent murder
by Hagen in the "Otten waldt" (Odenwald, 177.8).[8]

*Das Lied vom Hürnen Seyfrid,* which Eugen Mogk, in his inaugural
lecture at the University of Leipzig in 1895, had referred to as a
"Bänkelsängerlied" ("balladmonger's tune"), can scarcely be compared with the *Nibelungenlied* in terms of literary merit. Scholars are
not at all sure whether the poem is actually a combination of several
independent lays, as Wilhelm Grimm suggested,[9] or the work of
one author. Its importance, however, within the literary tradition

of the *Nibelungen* is summed up by King in the excellent introduction to his edition:

However one looks at the poem it is undeniable that it tells us things about Siegfried which the other sources we know do not tell us; and these things are of interest whether they can be traced back to Germanic antiquity or not, for it is just as important for the history of literature to know whether an ancient popular hero remained merely an ancient popular hero or whether he continued to occupy a significant position in the creative literature of later times. [10]

Relying to a large degree on *Das Lied vom Hürnen Seyfrid* as a base, Hans Sachs completed, in 1557, his tragedy in seven acts, *Der Hürnen Seufrid* (Sewfrid, the Dragon-Slayer), and thus became the first writer to adapt a segment of the *Nibelungen* tradition for the stage. The *Lied* serves as a basis for the first five acts of the play, while the preparations for the fight between Sewfrid and Dietrich, as well as the actual combat (acts 6 and 7), appear to be based on a work from the late thirteenth century, *Der grosse Rosengarten*. It is impossible to ascertain whether Hans Sachs knew the *Nibelungenlied*, although most scholars are inclined to doubt that this was the case.

As in the *Lied*, Sewfrid, son of Sigmund, is not given to courtly mores and, from the outset, demonstrates a high degree of haughtiness. He is "gar vnadelicher art" ("certainly not noble in bearing"),[11] "frech, verwegen vnd muetwillig" ("haughty, daring, and headstrong").[12] Acts 3 through 5 deal with the abduction of Crimhilt by the dragon and Sewfrid's adventures in the process of rescuing her. When, in act 5, Sewfrid learns from the dwarf that he will only be granted eight years together with Crimhilt, he accepts it as "God's will" (747; note also 900!). Acts 6 and 7 are of particular interest to us. In the former, Crimhilt is depicted as an ambitious woman, eager to see how Sewfrid would fare in battle against Dietrich, and quite conscious of the universal fame he will attain should he prove triumphant (note 896f.). Significantly, *vbermuet* (*Übermut*, "haughtiness," "arrogance") is singled out in 870 as a trait from which nothing good can come. In the contest which follows, Dietrich eventually proves to be too formidable for Sewfrid, who flees to Crimhilt and seeks refuge in her lap! This is a very different image of the hero as compared to the way Siegfried was portrayed in earlier sources, as well as in later works. The final act of Sachs's

tragedy relates the murder of Sewfrid by Hagen who, in 1068f,
gives some idea of the motivation behing the deed: "Nun hat auch
ain ent dein hochmuet, / Der vns fort nit mer irren thuet" ("Now
your arrogance has come to an end, and will no longer give us cause
to worry"; compare strophe 993 in the Nibelungenlied!).[13]

The *Wunderschöne Historia von dem gehörnten Siegfried* (The mar-
velous story of Siegfried, the Dragon-Slayer), commonly dated from
1726,[14] the year of the earliest surviving edition, had its origins as
a printed folk book almost seventy years earlier, as Harold Jantz
has shown in his delightful and informative essay, "The Last Branch
of the Nibelungen Tree."[15] Like its poetic forerunner, the prose
*Historia* relates the story of Siegfried, here the son of King Sieghardus
of the Netherlands, a tall, muscular young man, whose urge for
independence causes his parents some anxiety. Even though the
king's advisers suggest that the prince be allowed to make his way
in the world, Siegfried takes his leave unannounced. After a brief
encounter with a smith, whom he antagonizes with his arrogance
and brute strength, Siegfried slays a dragon in a nearby forest and
burns him, using the fat which is produced to toughen (*hürnen*) his
skin. The greater part of the folk book is devoted to the story of
Siegfried's rescue of Florigunda, daughter of King Gilbaldus of
Worms, from a dragon. As in the *Lied* and the play, prince and
princess wed, but Siegfried incurs the jealousy of his three brothers-
in-law because he consistently wins the prizes offered in tournaments. He is eventually killed by one of the trio, Hagenwald, and
is avenged by his father, Sieghardus. The folk book closes with an
allusion to Löwhardus, Siegfried's son, who, it is said, grew up to
be a fine hero.[16]

In many respects, the *Historia* is simply a prose rendition of the
late-fifteenth-century *Lied*. Siegfried is portrayed, however, as a
Christian knight; and, as in the *Lied,* there is no attempt to depict
the heroine, Florigunda, as the avenging she-devil, an image which
would scarcely have found much sympathetic reception in the early
seventeenth century.

## The Nineteenth Century

Throughout the remainder of the seventeenth and most of the
eighteenth century, the subject matter of the *Nibelungen* provided
no incentive for further literary productions among German authors.

With the advent of romanticism and the national fervor which swept through the country at the time of the Napoleonic Wars, enthusiasm for the German past in general and the Middle Ages in particular increased among poets as well as scholars. The effort to free Germany and Europe from Napoleon's armies was complemented by the attempt to use the *Nibelungenlied* for political purposes. Siegfried, the dragon-slayer, came to be regarded as a national hero, the German Achilles. Ludwig Tieck's ballads, "Siegfrieds Jugend" (Siegfried's Youth) and "Siegfried der Drachentödter" (Siegfried the Dragon-Slayer, 1804), concentrate on the early life of the hero, although the second poem also alludes to his death. Tieck does not ignore Siegfried's *übermuot,* but in "Siegfried der Drachentödter" that word assumes a more positive quality than is the case in either the *Nibelungenlied* or the *Lied vom Hürnen Seyfrid.* Ludwig Uhland composed a poem in rhyming couplets with Siegfried as the central figure, "Siegfrieds Schwert" (Siegfried's sword, 1812), and the prominent translator of the *Nibelungenlied,* Karl Simrock, produced a ballad entitled "Der Nibelungen-Hort" (The treasure of the Nibelungs, 1827). The popularity of lyric and epic renditions of the *Nibelungen* theme was extraordinary throughout the nineteenth century,[17] but it was in drama where, more than anywhere else, the extent to which the material had captured the imagination of contemporary authors was demonstrated.

In particular, one witnesses a veritable proliferation of *Nibelungenlied* dramas which reflect, in chronological sequence, the spirit of the Wars of Liberation against Napoleon, the national movements of the mid-nineteenth century (especially the Revolution of 1848), and the nationalistic tendencies prevalent at the time of the founding of the Second Reich by Bismarck (1871). In his dissertation, *Der Nibelungenstoff auf dem deutschen Theater* (The *Nibelungen* theme on the German stage),[18] Holger Schulz lists no fewer than fourteen dramas which were produced between 1810 and 1861, including works by such noted authors as Ludwig Uhland, Geibel, Ibsen, and Hebbel.[19] Hebbel's trilogy *(Der gehörnte Siegfried* (Siegfried, the Dragon-Slayer), *Siegfrieds Tod* (Siegfried's death), *Kriemhilds Rache* (Kriemhild's Revenge), which I shall examine more closely, enjoyed considerable popularity on the German stage in the nineteenth and early twentieth centuries, but failed to exercise much influence on subsequent dramas. It was probably not fully understood, despite the number of successful productions it enjoyed.[20] Between 1866 and 1951,

Schulz lists a further twenty *Nibelungenlied* dramas, many of which, however, he designates as amateurish ("dilettantische Stücke").[21] Apart from dramas concerned with the theme of the *Nibelungenlied* in general, Schulz also cites a number of works dealing with individual figures (Rüdeger, Attila, Kudrun, Dietrich), as well as a few "Merovingian dramas," which accord with the efforts to link Merovingian history to the events depicted in the epic.

Although there was no lack of *Nibelungen* dramas throughout the nineteenth century, few managed to gain any lasting recognition. Gottfried Weber states: "Regardless of the reason, none of them ever attained the poetic stature of the medieval work."[22] Many were not received well on the stage, and, of the dozens which appeared in print, only Hebbel's *Nibelungen* is still read with any frequency today (the readers being primarily Germanists and their students). In his poem, "Sigurd unter den Gänsen" (Sigurd among the geese, 1839), Friedrich Rückert poked fun at the dilettantism inherent in many of the plays which used the *Nibelungenlied* as a source, falling over it "wie jugendliche Leser / oder wie ein Heer von Recensenten" ("like youthful readers or an army of critics").[23] In Heine's "Deutschland," Germany was compared to the brash, temperamental Siegfried whom we find in the *Lied vom Hürnen Seyfrid*. Felix Dahn's "Der Bundestag" (The federal parliament) utilized the treasure of the Nibelungs as a symbol of unity. In his "Deutsche Lieder" (German songs) Dahn compared the envisioned destruction of Germany at the hands of a Russian, French, and Italian coalition to the heroic demise of the Nibelungs in Attila's Great Hall.

Let us return for a while to Friedrich Hebbel's *Die Nibelungen: Ein deutsches Trauerspiel in drei Abteilungen* / (The Nibelungs: A German tragedy in three parts), for of all the plays produced during the nineteenth and twentieth centuries on this theme, it is the one that deserves more than fleeting mention. Hebbel's diary entry of 18 February 1857 alludes to a visit the dramatist paid to the home of Amalia Schoppen in Hamburg, at which time he became acquainted with the *Nibelungenlied* and was particularly impressed by the figures. In Vienna, Hebbel attended a performance of Ernst Raupach's *Der Nibelungenhort* (The treasure of the Nibelungs, published 1834) and, in a letter to Charlotte Rousseau, he expressed his delight with Christine Enghaus (whom he later married) in the role of Chriemhild. Hebbel's drama was conceived over a period of five years, from 1855 to 1860, during which time he familiarized himself with the renditions of previous authors. He was aware of the difficulties inherent in such a project, the most prominent being the transposing of epic figures onto the stage,[24] but he believed that the *Nibelungenlied* poet had been a "dramatist from his head to his toes."[25]

The *Nibelungen* consists of three parts: *Der gehörnte Siegfried: Vorspiel in einem Akt*, *Siegfrieds Tod*, and *Kriemhilds Rache*. Under the influence of Friedrich Theodor Vischer, Hebbel attempted to produce a drama in conformity with the latter's call for a logical justification of every action undertaken by psychologically unified characters. Members of human society (in contrast to those figures whose origins lay in the supernatural sphere) were to be depicted as acting from a position of complete independence and would bear full responsibility for their actions.[26] In *Der gehörnte Siegfried*, Hebbel retains much of the arrogance we associate with Siegfried upon his arrival in Worms: "Ich grüss dich, König Gunther von Burgund!— / Du staunst, dass du den Siegfried bei dir siehst? / Er kommt, mit dir zu kämpfen um dein Reich!" ("I greet you, King Gunther of Burgundy. You are amazed to see Siegfried here before you? I have come to fight you for your empire.")[27] We are also made aware of Gunther's overestimation of his talents. Upon hearing of the danger for Brünhild's suitors and the fate of those who have hitherto attempted to woo her, the king exclaims that this can only prove that she is intended for him. As in the *Nibelungenlied*, a deal is fashioned whereby Siegfried agrees to procure Brünhild (who, he maintains, has not touched his heart) for Gunther if he can wed Kriemhild in return. Siegfried has thus been clearly identified with a world set far apart from that of the court at Worms. The ominous predictions regarding the outcome of the wooing mission are delivered by Volker: "Nein, König, bleib daheim / Es endet schlecht" ("No, my king, remain at home. This will turn out badly").[28] Volker recognizes the deeper significance in what is proposed, and maintains that "falsche Künste" ("magic") are not appropriate to the Burgundians.

In *Siegfrieds Tod*, Hebbel places Brünhild squarely into the foreground and, in a scene reminiscent of the arrival of the Burgundians in Iceland in the *Nibelungenlied*, allows her to address Siegfried first in the assumption that it is he who has come to woo her. He devotes no time to the actual ordeals in which Gunther-Siegfried must prove victorious in order to obtain Brünhild, but quickly moves the scene from Isenland and Brünhild's castle to Worms and Gunther's palace.

It is Hagen who makes the initial suggestion that Siegfried "tame" Brünhild in bed, claiming that the honor of the king is at stake. In contrast to the situation in the *Nibelungenlied,* Siegfried is less than willing to comply with the request. His eventual acquiescence, coupled with his indiscretion in taking Brünhild's girdle, leads to the subsequent confrontation between Brünhild, conscious of her status as queen of the Burgundians, and Kriemhild, to whom Siegfried is "the strongest man in the world." When Hagen states that Siegfried must die, his motives go beyond those of his counterpart in the *Nibelungenlied.* It is not just a question of jealousy and dislike or, for that matter, fear of the hero. Siegfried is not simply the "Schwätzer" ("prattler"). Hagen recognizes that there is more than hate perceived by Brünhild toward Siegfried. They are of the same world, inescapably drawn to one another by their very nature; theirs is a magical bond that can only be dissolved by death:

> "Ein Zauber ists,
> Durch den sich ihr Geschlecht erhalten will,
> Und der die letzte Riesin ohne Lust
> Wie ohne Wahl zum letzten Riesen treibt."
>                         (act 4, scene 9)

("It is magic, by means of which their race attempts to survive, and which draws the last giantess—neither by choice, nor by desire—to the last giant.")

Kriemhild is modeled closely on her counterpart in the *Nibelungenlied,* and, in *Kriemhilds Rache,* Hebbel also allows her to degenerate into a dark figure who would "cut down a hundred brothers" (act 4, scene 4) in order to get Hagen's head. As in the medieval forerunner, the Burgundian kings are in no way inclined to give in to Kriemhild's offer that they may leave Attila's court unharmed after turning over Hagen. Lifted from the *Nibelungenlied* as well are Rüdeger's plight (act 5, scene 11) and the final confrontation between Hagen and Kriemhild, including a contemporary version of the original appellative hurled at Kriemhild by Hagen, "Unhold" ("devil," act 5, scene 14). Similarly, Hagen dies by Kriemhild's hand, and the queen is struck down by Hildebrand, who refers to her as a devil. In contrast to the *Nibelungenlied,* however, Hebbel's drama concludes with Attila's abdication and Dietrich's acceptance of his crown "in the name of the one who died on the cross" (act 5, scene 14).

What had Hebbel intended with the *Nibelungen?* In a short essay entitled "An den geneigten Leser" (To the sympathetic reader), he expressed his desire to adapt "the dramatic treasure of the Nibelungenlied"[29] for the stage. The actions of the characters were to be their own, that is, independent of the influence of superhuman beings. While Hebbel urged his readers to seek nothing more than the "Nibelungen Not" behind this tragedy, he clearly offered a three-phrase development from the mythical, through the heathen, to the Christian era. In marked contrast to the *Nibelungenlied,* where no future is envisioned, Hebbel's *Nibelungen,* while not conveying in the final words of Dietrich (who represents the antithesis of the demonic Hagen) the idea of a "crawling to the cross,"[30] offers an affirmation of a new life, a new beginning, and thus endows the work with a very different spirit when compared with that of its medieval forerunner.

The patriotic fervor engendered by the Franco-Prussian War of 1870–71 led to a glorification of conflict and lent emphasis to the concepts of unity, strength, and loyalty. Emanuel Geibel's poem, "An Deutschland. Januar 1871" (To Germany, January, 1871) contained a reference to the "marrow of the Nibelungs," and Julius Rodenberg's "Die Heimkehr" (The homecoming, 1872), a tribute to Wilhelm I, referred to the Kaiser as the "Sieg-Fried" of the German people. All of Germany became a "Nibelungenland" (Adolf Bartels, 1896) in the last years of the nineteenth century, and the Germans themselves were depicted as the "Nibelungenstamm," "the Nibelungen clan." Bismarck, the "Iron Chancellor" and engineer of German unity in the last half of the nineteenth century, was also compared to Siegfried in Felix Dahn's poems "Jung-Bismarck" (Young Bismarck) and "Bei Bismarcks Tod" (On Bismarck's death). This symbolism became even more pronounced in Hermann Hoffmeister's "Der eiserne Siegfried" (Iron Siegfried), where Bismarck was compared to the hero of Xanten, and Fafnir, the slain dragon, to the threatening "Sozialdemokratismus" which was becoming more and more noticeable throughout the land.

The *Nibelungen* theme inspired not only literary productions in the nineteenth century. Vischer, whose influence on Hebbel has been noted above, was the first to attempt the production of an opera based on the subject ("Vorschlag zu einer Oper" [Suggestion for an opera, 1844]), and he was followed by Louise Otto (*Die Nibelungen als Oper,* [The Nibelungen as opera, 1845]), the Dane

Nils Wilhelm Gade (*Siegfried und Brynhilde,* 1847, a fragment), and
Heinrich Dorn (*Die Nibelungen,* 1854). In 1874, Richard Wagner
completed his tetralogy, *Der Ring des Nibelungen* (*The Ring of the
Nibelungen*), consisting of the *Vorabend, Das Rheingold* (*Prelude, Rhine
Gold,* 1854), and the three music dramas, *Die Walküre* (*The Val-
kyries,* 1856), *Siegfried* (1871), and *Götterdämmerung* (*Twilight of the
Gods,* 1874). The first complete performance of the *Ring* was given
in August 1876 in Bayreuth. In a letter to Franz Müller in Weimar,
dated 9 January 1855, Wagner referred to the sources he had consulted, ranging from Lachmann's *Nibelungen Noth und Klage,* through
the *Edda, Völsunga Saga, Wilkina-* and *Niflunga Saga,* to secondary
literature such as F. Joseph Mone's *Untersuchungen zur deutschen Heldensage* (Studies on German heroic poetry), which he considered to
be very important. Wagner was not concerned about remaining
"true" to the sources; he used them freely, deriving most of his
material from the *Edda* and the *Völsunga Saga.* His chief interest
lay in the mythical aspects of the material, and he did not bother
with the destruction of the Burgundians. The *Rheingold,* in fact, is
devoid of purely human characters. Brünhild is a central figure while
Gutrune (Kriemhild) is reduced to fulfilling a necessary dramatic
function. The *Ring* also betrays the influence of classical tragedy
and myth, and the tetralogy may be described as a veritable potpourri
of Germanic motifs, Christianity, Greek myth, and humanism.

Wagner also emphasizes the animosity perceived by Hagen toward
Siegfried and Brünhild. He is jealous of the former and also despises
him. Hagen deliberates; Siegfried acts. Hagen is conscious of the
significance of events transpiring around him; Siegfried, although
free, remains naive, oblivious to the ultimate meaning of his actions.
Unlike Siegfried, who openly admits that he often forgets the ring
of the Nibelungs and the treasure, Hagen's aim in life is directed
toward procuring the former.

Vischer maintained that, owing to the stature and archaism of
its figures, a dramatization of the *Nibelungen* theme was impossible.
Wagner contradicted Vischer in a most impressive manner, although
in his own time, it was by no means certain that his tetralogy would
enjoy the critical acclaim it does today. Writing of the first English
performance of the *Ring* in the *Era* of 13 May 1882, the music critic
concluded: "That the *Nibelungen Ring,* in spite of its occasional power
and beauty, can ever be popular, is more than we expect and certainly
more than we hope for."[31]

## The Twentieth Century

There is no radical break with tradition in *Nibelungenlied* reception during the early twentieth century. According to Werner Wunderlich,[32] three basic "types of reception" can be discerned: (1) Siegfried is portrayed as the young, carefree hero, whose foremost attributes are courage and loyalty; (2) the work and its figures are regarded from a mythical perspective, with Siegfried depicted as a symbol of "light" in contrast to his antagonists, who represent the "dark" side of existence; (3) the work is cited as an attempt to convey the image of "higher man," with both Siegfried and Brünhild regarded as exemplary. Intrinsic to this third type was the existential necessity of the hero's demise. In 1909, Paul Ernst, whom Ernst Alker has described as the "most important representative of neoclassicism,"[33] produced his demonic drama, *Brunhild* (followed, in 1918, by *Chriemhild*), in which he attempted through the use of expressionistic devices to move away from a Hebbel-like "Psychologisierung" ("psychologizing") of the characters and present the myth of the "higher man" and the ultimate tragedy of an existence which attained perfection only through its own demise. Ernst's drama had yet another function to fulfill, however, as the author himself indicated in his "Nachwort zu Chriemhild": "If something of the pride of the German has been expressed in my work, pride which he may now be accorded at the time of his great humiliation, then I shall be happy, for I will thus have fulfilled my obligation as a poet."[34] Siegfried and Brünhild are portrayed as "outsiders," as beings set apart from the rest of society, "higher entities," whose very nature cannot help but bring them into conflict with the world about them. Although they ideally should serve as models for "lower men," such as Gunther and Kriemhild, the manner in which they are abused by the latter leads to their tragic demise.[35] The question of guilt is not pertinent in Ernst's dramas. Fate is decisive, and it lies in the nature of the hero to behave as a demigod, trapped by his insistence on coming to terms with the world of "lower men," with release possible only in death. When Ernst's Hagen, whom the author viewed as a "figure of depth, strength, greatness, and tragedy,"[36] decides that Siegfried must die, he acts from higher necessity, knowing full well that Gunther and Khriemhild are the "cancer" in society.[37]

World War I produced a further utilization of the *Nibelungenlied*
in the service of the country, an identification of main characters
in the medieval epic with specific German traits or institutions.
Siegfried was viewed as a symbol of military strength and was
compared to both Germany and the German army. At the beginning
of the war this was also true for Hagen, although he later became
associated with the "stab-in-the-back" theory advanced by many in
the postwar period.[38] Wilhelm Scherer ("Nibelungentreue: Kriegs-
gesänge" [Nibelung loyalty: war songs, 1916]) conjured up the
image of a reincarnated Siegfried representing strength and loyalty,
and Werner Jansen dedicated his novel *Das Buch Treue: Nibelungen-
roman* (The book of loyalty: A Nibelung novel, 1921) to the German
war dead, the memory of whose heroism and loyalty had given him
the courage to bring his work to its conclusion. When the war was
lost and the Weimar Republic founded, conservative opponents of
the regime turned to the *Nibelungenlied* as a model in their call for
Germany's renewal, for, if models were indeed to be found, one
need look no further than to the "national epic." Friedrich Vogt,
in a reference to "Nibelungentreue" ("Nibelung loyalty"), compared
the endurance demonstrated by the Burgundians in the burning
palace of Attila to Germany's will to resist the enemy coalitions of
World War I (*Französischer und deutscher Nationalgeist im Rolandslied
und im Nibelungenlied* [French and German national spirit in the lay
of Roland and the Nibelungenlied, 1922]).

The *Nibelungen* theme found warm reception in National Socialist
Germany between 1933 and 1945. Wunderlich contrasts the different perspectives from which the material was viewed. During the
Weimar Republic, the themes and motifs of the *Nibelungenlied* had
been employed by authors of antirepublican persuasion to express
optimism for Germany's future, but poets and dramatists sympathetic to the Third Reich spoke in terms of the present. Siegfried
was seen by some as the prototype of Nordic man, as the embodiment
of the Nordic spirit. His fate was compared with that of the Germanic race. In "Das Lied von Siegfried" (The lay of Siegfried, 1934),
Hans Henning von Grote portrayed Siegfried, the dragon-slayer, as
the destroyer of dark forces, the personification of loyalty and the
ever-recurring hero in times of peril. The identification of Siegfried
with Arminius was revitalized by Bodo Ernst in his *Siegfried-Armin:
Der Mythos vom deutschen Menschen* (Siegfried-Arminius: The myth of
the German, 1935) and Paul Albrecht in *Arminius-Sigurfrid: Ein*

*Roman des deutschen Volkes* (Arminius-Siegfried: A novel of the German people, 1935). Ernst Huttig's *Siegfried: Festliches Spiel in drei dramatischen Szenen und zwei Bühnenbildern* (Siegfried: A festive play in three dramatic scenes and two stage scenes, 1934) depicts the hero as a selfless warrior in the service of others, comparable to Germany and the role of its soldiers in foreign service throughout the world in previous centuries. Similar thoughts were echoed by Karl Busch in *Das Nibelungenlied in deutscher Geschichte und Kunst* (The Nibelungenlied in German history and art, 1934). Josef Weinheber's poem "Siegfried-Hagen" (1936) compares the perilous situation of the "blond-haired hero," murdered among his "friends," with that of the Reich, which the poet considers in danger of collapsing as a result of inner strife and lack of harmony. But Hagen, too, could be portrayed as the "personification of the Nordic type,"[39] as in Wulf Bley's play *Die Gibichunge* (The Gibechs, 1934), in which the hero of Troneck maintains that it was his destiny to kill Siegfried.[40] Throughout this period in Germany, the *Nibelungenlied* was regarded as a work which reflected "the historical mission of the German people and the natural and necessary battle for existence of the individual as well as the race, or the people."[41] The Nibelungs were considered the epitome of courage, prowess in battle, and, above all, loyalty, both to the people and its leader. With the outbreak of World War II, the bellicose tendencies of individuals and peoples in the *Nibelungenlied,* the spirit of the warrior, became prime models for a new generation of soldiers.[42] As the military victories of the years 1939 to 1942 gave way to the defeats of 1943 to 1945, the emphasis was placed more on the fatalistic acceptance of catastrophe, of defiance in the face of death and total destruction. To die was not important; to die with honor in a heroic struggle, as the Nibelungs had done, was paramount. War was considered the test of heroic man, that which ultimately gave meaning to one's existence, a theme which was prominent in Hans Baumann's *Rüdiger von Bechelaren: Das Passauer Nibelungenspiel* (Rüdeger of Bechelaren: Passau's Nibelung play, 1939).

The postwar period evinced two major phases in the reception of the *Nibelungenlied* in Germany.[43] On the one hand, there was a concerted effort to move away from the trends of earlier periods, while, on the other, some of the old concepts and interpretations continued to be propagated. In 1944, the production of the first part of Max Mell's drama, *Der Nibelunge Not* (The tragedy of the

Nibelungs), took place in Vienna. The second part, *Kriemhilds Rache,* was performed six years later. Mell attempted to move away from titanic concepts and, while accentuating Christian ethics in his work, depicted the Nibelungs as human beings. In two tragedies, *Siegfried* and *Grimhild* (1948), Wilhelm Hildebrand Schäfer depicted the world as a stage on which Siegfried, the visionary, a superior man, is destroyed by the narrow-mindedness of society and its pragmatic outlook. Reinhold Schneider's play, *Tarnkappe* (The magic cloak, 1951), is rooted in the Christian-humanistic tradition,and portrays the constant struggle faced by the individual to realize a Christian existence in this life.

In the 1950s, the theme of the *Nibelungen* fell prey to *Trivialliteratur* and pornography. In the comic series, *Sigurd,* Siegfried appears as a German Tarzan or Superman, and the figure was sexually exploited in the 1969 film *Siegfried und das sagenhafte Liebesleben der Nibelungen* (Siegfried and the fabulous love life of the Nibelungs). (Compare, however, the skill with which the subject had been treated in the 1920s in the expressionistic films of Fritz Lang.) Crude sexual symbolism also characterized the 1961 novel by Martin Beheim-Schwarzbach, *Der Stern von Burgund: Roman der Nibelungen* (The star of Burgundy: A novel of the Nibelungs). What has appeared over the past twenty-five years in the Federal Republic of Germany utilizing the *Nibelungen* theme has been almost exclusively satirical in nature.[44] Robert Neumann's *Sperrfeuer um Deutschland* (Germany under Siege, 1950) and *Das Buch Treue: Ein Domelanen-Roman* (The book of loyalty: A novel of the Domelans, 1962) parodied both the concept of *Nibelungentreue* as well as the works of prior generations of authors who had adapted the theme. Joachim Fernau's *Disteln für Hagen: Bestandsaufnahme der deutschen Seele* (third edition, 1966) is a satirical retelling of the *Nibelungenlied* with the ambitious goal of determining the essence of the German mind. Axel Plogsted's play, *Die Nibelungen* (1975), and Beda Odemann's *Alles bebt vor Onkel Hagen: Ein Verhohnepiepel der deutschen "Heldensage"* (Everyone's frightened of Uncle Hagen: A satire on German heroic poetry) demonstrate that few contemporary authors who deal with the *Nibelungen* topic are as concerned with the aesthetics of their "literary" products as they are with parodying the concepts (particularly loyalty and heroism) which are of major significance in the medieval work. In this respect, they have become rather predictable, and, unfortunately, often tedious. In contrast, Franz Fühmann (German Democratic

Republic) has regarded the *Nibelungenlied* as a "novel about feudal society and its power structures,"[45] and has attempted in his poem "Der Nibelunge Not" (1956) to explain recent German history and provide a vision for the future. The optimistic tenor of the concluding strophes of Fühmann's poem stands in marked contrast to the apocalyptic conclusion of the medieval epic.

We shall close this chapter with an allusion to the popular interest demonstrated over the past few years in determining the historical and geographical background of the epic. Helmut Berndt's *Das 40. Abenteuer: Auf den Spuren der Nibelungen* (The Fortieth Adventure: Tracking the Nibelungs, 1964, with numerous subsequent editions) still adhered to the "traditional" route of the Burgundians from Worms on the Rhine through Bavaria and Austria to Hungary. In the summer of 1981, two new works appeared disputing the hitherto prevailing view that the Burgundians had actually journeyed to Hungary, or that the Nibelung treasure was sunk in the Rhine near Worms. The titles of both books in themselves betray the "new" direction of historically oriented lay studies: Heinz Ritter Schaumburg, *Die Nibelungen zogen nordwärts* (The Nibelungs went north), and Walter Böckmann, *Der Nibelungen Tod in Soest* (The demise of the Nibelungs in Soest). Well might we query with Werner Wunderlich: "The beginnings of a new myth?"[46]

## Chapter Six
# Concluding Remarks

In an age grown cynical toward concepts such as honor, loyalty, and courage, it is intriguing to note that the *Nibelungenlied,* whether taught in an undergraduate survey course or a graduate seminar, continues to stir the imagination of students and stimulates debate on issues that, on another level, are also the substance of many contemporary scholarly publications. Some of the attraction the epic holds may lie in its uniqueness. At a time when Arthurian poets presented their audiences with tales which underscored the inevitability of ultimate harmony and peace, when Walther and Reinmar sang their praises of women and the joy of love, or Hartmann von Aue provided a happy end for poor sinners, the *Nibelungenlied* poet offered a grim picture of individual depravity and mass destruction, a world gone mad, with no consoling words for a more positive future.

Was he simply a pessimist, a fatalist, a self-proclaimed soothsayer anxious to make a statement about the society he knew or man in general? However we may regard him, the author of our poem had a sense for tragedy unmatched by any of his contemporaries, combined with a remarkable talent for portraying a cataclysmic series of events without feeling obliged to resort to a "black and white" framework in the depiction of his main characters.

At the conclusion of his excellent monograph on Siegfried scholarship, Werner Hoffmann has remarked that there is no *one* image of Siegfried which has been conveyed by scholars,[1] and the same must be said for the interpretation of the *Nibelungenlied,* both as a complete work and with regard to any number of its components. No interpretation of the epic may lay claim to exclusivity. Yet anyone who writes on the subject is obliged to take a position on particular issues, and must also come to terms with the overall significance of the poem. With respect to the latter, I regard the *Nibelungenlied* less as a warning intended by the poet for a specific social group or a condemnation of a particular societal structure prevailing in Germany at the turn of the thirteenth century than as a general declaration (not judgment) of man's condition, a poignant message concerning the illusory nature of *vreude* ("joy"). It is most likely the testament of a confirmed pessimist, as the narrator's words in 2378.4 would tend to substantiate: "als ie diu liebe leide z'aller jungeste gît" ("just as joy always turns to sorrow in the end"; note also Kriemhild's words in 17.3). In contrast to the author of the *Klage,* who allowed Brünhild and the surviving Burgundians to find consolation in the crowning of the young prince Siegfried, Gunther's only son, and who thus left a door open for renewed hope in the future and the restoration of harmony, the *Nibelungenlied* poet is decidedly nihilistic. There is no help, no consolation, either in this world or in the next. Man is alone, but in this solitariness there is manifest greatness, as individual heroes face an irrevocable fate with composure and dignity.

Many questions which have been merely touched upon in this monograph deserve further attention. Scholars have argued for years about "Christianity" and "Paganism" in the *Nibelungenlied.* The Christian God and Heaven are to be found documented throughout the epic and even Hagen makes reference to them. But the use of such terms is formal and often formulaic. Christianity without depth and substance is, however, a contradiction in terms. The *Nibelungenlied* is hardly intended to convey a religious message. The poet has most assuredly made use of the religious terminology of his time, but he has never exploited the basic tenets of Christianity to provide his readers with a rebuttal to the *Sittenkodex* ("ethical code") of the Burgundians as they face death in Hungary. Nor is the question of Siegfried's murder even dealt with from the perspective of Christianity. (Those who consider both Rüdeger and Dietrich to be idealized representatives of Christianity in the epic do not explain how these knights can accept the murderer Hagen with such open arms, on no occasion even hinting at the moral ramifications of his act.) But if the *Nibelungenlied* is not intended as a Christian work, it is just as certainly not a conscious affirmation of "pre- (and even anti-) Christian" ideals and ideas. Heathenism and Christianity are not mutually exclusive to the poet, for he does not approach his material from a theological point of view.[2] The mingling of Christian and non-Christian knights at the court of Attila may reflect his sentiments in this respect. The theological dichotomy does not concern the poet at all. In the *Nibelungenlied,* Christian influence is not synonymous with Christian spirit. Bert Nagel may be quite correct when he maintains that, because of his position within society, the poet was undoubtedly "sympathetic toward the Church,"[3] but this, if we are to judge by the Christian references in the *Nibelungenlied*, may be more a concession to the temper of the time than a confirmation of his own piety.

On the matter of "individuals" and "types," I would concur with Hoffmann, Schröder, and Nagel, among others, that we are dealing here with more than stereotyped figures.[4] Can anyone seriously question the uniqueness of either Kriemhild or Hagen? We are not maintaining, of course, that the poet has endowed them with modern psychological profiles as one might expect of characters in late nineteenth- and twentieth-century novels. The character of Kriemhild has been skillfully molded; she is the element around which the unity of the epic revolves and the *Nibelungenlied* is, for the most part, the story of Kriemhild. (One might conceivably argue that it is also the tale of the Burgundians, their relationship to Siegfried, their killing of the hero, their isolation of Kriemhild, and their subsequent downfall.) From the outset, the poet has underscored the basic dichotomy between Kriemhild and the society in which she is raised. The reader is offered insight into her ever-increasing isolation, her "development" from a beautiful princess (albeit with a penchant for egocentricity and *übermuot*) into a *vâlandinne*, the demonic mistress of the Other World. Kriemhild's degeneration into a monster is considered by the poet as the prime reason for the calamity which befalls both Burgundians and Huns. At the same time, however, he does not ignore, despite his apparent sympathy for the figure, the demonic side of Hagen. The latter makes it abundantly clear on a number of occasions that he is the real protector of the Burgundian dynasty. His loyalty, in a higher sense, is to the line, not the ruling individuals, and yet he is largely responsible for the slaughter of the major part of his people.

One of the most difficult questions facing the literary critic or interpreter of a literary work is that of "literary merit." We are not simply referring here to the appeal a specific work may exercise on subsequent generations of readers, but also to the problem of establishing a valid set of criteria for arriving at a judgment concerning its intrinsic value. Modern readers are not in the position of the guild members who judged the performances of the *Meistersinger* in the fifteenth and sixteenth centuries in accordance with a predetermined set of rules and a set format. For the literature of the German

High Middle Ages, there is no standard to which an author must adhere other than the purely formal matter of meter and rhyme. The length of works may vary, and there is room for considerable flexibility with regard to the classical unity of time, place, and action. Judged by the standards of the later *Meistersinger,* the "[i]nconsistencies, [o]bscurities, and [p]revarications" of the *Nibelungenlied* poet would prove a formidable hindrance to according him merit as an author of repute.[5] The flaws are certainly real, yet they have not caused the poem to be ignored or to vanish into obscurity. What, then, has kept the *Nibelungenlied* an object of attraction for generations of scholars and laymen alike, and what are the merits of the poem which have occasioned A. T. Hatto to remark that it "is the world's best heroic epic bar one?"[6]

Hatto offers as a basis for this judgment the "strength, vitality, and tension of the *Nibelungenlied.*"[7] I would agree completely with his choice of criteria, all of which pertain to the "inner worth" of the poem. These are qualities which characterize more the substance of the *Nibelungenlied* than its form (although, as we have seen, the poet could be quite adept at combining formal stylistic devices with content to achieve a maximum of vitality and strength of expression). Nagel has also maintained that "when a poem with archaic content, such as the *Nibelungenlied,* can even today exert a broad influence, this is due to the vital inner force given it by the poet, a force that has not been exhausted."[8] The epic evinces the author's talent for portraying human beings, their motivations, emotions, and actions, in terms which are "universal" in the sense that they transcend the time in which the work was written down. The sensitive reader of today can still gain an appreciation of the dilemma faced by individuals within the poem and the extent to which their adherence to absolutes can lead to the collapse of their worlds. The theme of man, that "durch sich selber gefährdete Mensch" ("endangered by his own acts"),[9] is not only of significance for the literary world of 1200, but also that of the 1980s.

# Appendix A:
# The *Nibelungen* Tradition in Scandinavia

The *Nibelungenlied* represents only one, although perhaps the most significant, literary link in the *Nibelungen* tradition. While we cannot speculate here on the possible direct connections between the German epic and the analogues in Scandinavia, a brief overview of the latter may help the lay reader to understand the position of the *Nibelungenlied* within this tradition. There is no attempt to construct a "Stammbaum" as Heusler has done. We have simply begun with the premise that the "raw material" of the work, its *Stoff,* was not the original product of the imagination of our poet. By that we do not mean, of course, to denigrate the achievement of the author, but rather wish to emphasize that his materials had been in circulation for some time prior to the point at which he employed them in a uniquely individual fashion to produce his masterpiece.

The *Nibelungen* theme was especially popular in Scandinavia. Within the literature that has survived, we can distinguish four major thematic groups: (1) the adventures of Young Siegfried, (2) the death of Siegfried, (3) the destruction of the Burgundians, and (4) the end of Attila. Groups 2 and 3 form the nucleus of the *Nibelungenlied* itself, while 1 and 4 are accorded only the most peripheral treatment by the poet.

In the following pages, I shall confine myself to a brief description of six literary analogues which show certain thematic similarities to the *Nibelungenlied.* Four of these are lays, contained within the *Sae-mundar-Edda,* or *Older Edda.* The *Edda,* a collection of heroic and mythological lays whose origins extend from the ninth to the thirteenth century, was written down in Iceland about the year 1250.[1]

## *Brot af Sigurparkvidu (Fragment of a Sigurth Lay)*

This fragment of twenty-odd stanzas constitutes a part of the conclusion of a lay concerning Sigurth (Siegfried). What must be reconstructed are the events which lead up to and occasion the decision on the part of Gunnar (Gunther) to kill Sigurth. The fragment begins with a query by Högni (Hagen) as to the harm that Sigmund's son has done Gunnar. The latter replies that Sigurth is an oath-breaker, but it is not until the last stanza that we learn the nature of the oath sworn by Sigurth (not to violate Gunnar's wife) and that he did, in fact, remain true to it. Högni is depicted as a more perceptive individual than Gunnar, maintaining that the latter's wife, Brynhild, has been responsible for the hostility that Gunnar feels toward Sigurth. Jealousy, he claims, is the prime motive (stanza 3). Guthorm, who is not bound by an oath of fidelity to Sigurth, is engaged to murder the hero. No details of the actual deed are provided, but the succinct narration of the act is simultaneously complemented by an allusion to the subsequent death of Gunnar and Högni at the hands of Attila:

> Slain was Sigurth, south of the Rhine.
> A raven on tree had wrathfully cawed:
> "Atli's sword blade your blood will redden,
> your mainsworn oaths will murder you."[2]

Brynhild offers a consoling word to the murderers, claiming that, had Sigurth lived, he would have laid claim to Gjúki's (father of Gunnar, Högni, Guthrún) lands and his treasure. (This may reflect anxieties similar to those alluded to in a more nebulous manner by Hagen in the *Nibelungenlied,* strophe 993.) Guthrún (Kriemhild in the *Nibelungenlied*) curses Gunnar for having her husband murdered, wishing "threefold revenge" (stanza 11) upon him. The portents are not good; apart from the raven's prediction and Guthrún's curse, Brynhild has a dream in which Gunnar appears as a captive among his enemies. The fragment closes with a chiding Brynhild recalling the pact of friendship between Gunnar and Sigurth and making an allusion to the sword the hero had placed between himself and her on the nuptial bed, symbolizing his intention to adhere to his oath and leave her virginity intact. A short prose passage following the stanzas addresses the question of where Sigurth was killed; of importance to us is simply the statement that he was murdered in a treacherous manner.

In contrast to the *Nibelungenlied,* the *Brot* does not depict Gunnar as a weak king dominated by a strong liegeman. He is, however, not particularly perceptive and appears easily deceived by his wife.

The king is, in fact, the one who arrives at the decision to commit
the murder, and Högni implicitly advises against it. Brynhild's
motive for wanting Sigurth dead, if we are to believe Högni, was
jealousy, although Brynhild also alludes to the potential danger
Sigurth represented for Gunnar and the others. Like the *Nibelungenlied*, the lay contains dire predictions of what is to follow as a result
of Sigurth's death; by the very nature of its genre, however, there
is little room for a more extensive portrayal of his widow, Guthrún.
Brynhild's laugh subsequent to the killing (stanza 10) has a decidedly
demonic ring about it, and her sometimes sarcastic, chiding tone
in her admonishments of her husband endows her with characteristics
one would not normally associate with a queen. Implicit in the lay
is the fact that Sigurth, who rode through a wall of flame to fetch
Brynhild for Gunnar, was, in effect, the only true match for the
queen.

## *Sigurþarkvida hin skamma*
## *(The Short Lay of Sigurth)*

The *Sigurþarvida*, attributed to an Icelander of the eleventh or
twelfth century, consists of seventy stanzas which relate of Sigurth's
relationship to the sons of King Gjúki (Gunnar and Högni), his
marriage to their sister Guthrún, the assistance provided by Sigurth
in the procurement of Brynhild for Gunnar, and the subsequent
murder of the hero. Here, too, Sigurth is clearly the appropriate
match for Brynhild, but it is fate, according to the poet, which
keeps them apart. Brynhild is depicted as insanely jealous of Sigurth
and Guthrún. She urges Gunnar (through threats) to murder both
Sigurth and his son. When Gunnar summons Högni and inquires
if he would be willing to betray Sigurth, he mentions the "golden
rings," the sunken "hoard of the Rhine," as an incentive. Högni is
portrayed as a man of character who asserts that it would be dis-
honorable to betray their oaths for the sake of gold. Gunnar urges
Guthorm, who is not bound by oaths, to murder Sigurth, and he
does, in fact, slay him in bed. The remainder of the lay deals with
Brynhild and her preparations to join Sigurth in death, an act from
which Hagen refuses to restrain her. The lay also contains a prophecy
of Guthrún's subsequent fate.

## *Atlakvida (The Old Lay of Atli)*

The *Atlakvida*, the *Old Lay of Atli*, dates from the ninth century and relates of the fall of the Niflungs (Nibelungs). Consisting of forty-six stanzas with a short epic preface giving a précis of the lay, and a one-line epilogue referring to an expanded version *(Atlamál)*, the *Atlakvida* places Gunnar, brother of Guthrún and Högni, into the foreground and emphasizes the heroic stance exhibited by both Gunnar and Högni in the face of death at Atli's court. Atli, leader of the Huns, desires the treasure of the Niflungs, and for this reason extends an invitation to Gunnar to visit his court. Högni maintains, however, that there is treachery afoot, for they have received a ring from Guthrún, who is married to Atli, which has been wound with wolf's hair. Gunnar is depicted as a fearless hero whose sense of honor dictates that he must meet the challenge. Both he and Högni journey to Atli's court, where they are set upon and eventually killed. The heroic tenor of their deaths is unmistakable. Högni laughs defiantly as the Huns cut out his heart, while Gunnar strikes his harp as he awaits death in the snake pit. Guthrún exacts a terrible revenge for the murder of her brothers, first serving her two sons by Atli as a meal to the Hunnish leader, then killing him in his bed, and burning down the Great Hall, killing his men in the process. She herself subsequently dies.

There is much of the "demonic" in Guthrún, although she appears as a more sympathetic figure in the *Atlakvida* than does her counterpart Kriemhild in the *Nibelungenlied*. In contrast to the later epic, the lay does not allow death and destruction to reach the same proportions, culminating in the virtually total demise of Niflungs and Huns. While many of Atli's men perish in the burning hall, the slaughter is limited and one does not gain the impression that the world has come to an end.

## *Atlamál hin grœnlenzku (Greenlandish Lay of Atli)*

The *Atlamál*, or *Greenlandish lay of Atli*, is considered the work of an eleventh- or twelfth-century poet, and has been characterized, owing to its "repetitiousness, its lachrymose tone, its lack of breeding, its general air of 'a sad tale gone into song,' " as "a valuable foil and contrast to the nobel 'Atlakvida.' "[3] In essence, the *Atlamál* relates the same tale in ninety-six stanzas which is found in the *Atlakvida,* although in the former, Högni and Gunnar are advised by their wives, Kostbera (who interprets the runic warning sent by Guthrún) and Glaumvor, not to travel to Atli's court. Gunnar declares that they cannot escape their fate. As in the *Nibelungenlied,* there is a passage of water to traverse and, after having arrived on the other side, the Niflungs do not secure their boat, a symbolic act comparable to Hagen's destruction of the boat after having crossed the Danube in the *Nibelungenlied.* In the subsequent attack by the Huns on Gunnar and his small party, Guthrún picks up a sword and attempts to defend her brothers. Högni laughs as his heart is cut out, and Gunnar is also portrayed in an heroic stance at the moment of death. Atli's sons likewise meet a horrible end, with their brain-pans used as beakers for mead mixed with their blood, and their hearts served to Atli by Guthrún as though they were steaks. In the killing of Atli, however, Guthrún is assisted by Hniflung, Högni's son, and, in contrast to the *Atlakvida,* there is no mention of Guthrún's burning of the Great Hall. She herself is destined to live on for many a day.

## *Völsunga Saga*

The late thirteenth-century *Völsunga Saga* is a prose rendering of the Völsung poems contained within the *Elder Edda.* It makes extensive use of the *Sigurþarkvida hin skamma,* but combines the stories of Sigurth's death and Guthrún's Revenge (against Atli) in a manner quite distinct from that effected by the *Nibelungenlied* poet. The author of the *Völsunga Saga* provides a detailed description of Sigurd's youth, including his acquisition of the invincible sword Gram (a legacy from his father Sigmund, passed on in two pieces which are mended together by the smith Regin), his slaying of the Hundings, responsible for the death of his father, his killing of the worm (dragon) Fafnir, and his increased knowledge from contact with the blood of the latter. The relationship between Sigurd and Brynhild is explicit: awakened from a fairy-tale-like slumber by Sigurd, Brynhild shows herself to be exceedingly wise and knowledgeable. Although they pledge themselves to one another, Brynhild predicts that Sigurd will marry Gudrun, daughter of King Giuki, and sister of Gunnar, Högnir, and Gutthorm. This does, in fact, take place, for Grimhild, Gudrun's mother, offers Sigurd a magic drink which causes him to forget Brynhild. Grimhild also urges Gunnar to woo Brynhild, but it is only Sigurd, in the guise of Gunnar, who can cross through the wall of flame which surrounds her castle. He lies with her for three nights, but does not violate her; she gives him a ring before he departs. As in the *Nibelungenlied,* an argument later ensues between Brynhild and Gudrun (Kriemhild) over the question of status, and Gudrun gives away the secret that it was Sigurd who rode through the flaming wall and lay beside Brynhild for three nights. Brynhild lies to Gunnar about the three nights spent with Sigurd, implying that he was the one who robbed her of her virginity. She urges Gunnar to kill both Sigurd and his son, but Högni advises against it, citing both their oaths to Sigurd and the fact that he is a considerable asset to them. The hero is killed in bed by Gutthorm who, in turn, is struck down by Sigurd while trying to escape. Sigurd accepts his death as fate. Gunnar regrets that the act had to be carried out and Brynhild later admits that Sigurd had, in fact, held true to his oath and had not violated her. She dies and is burned by the side of Sigurd.

Once again, a magic potion is employed by the poet to overcome a thematic hurdle. Gudrun receives a drink from Gunnar which causes her to forget the guilt of her brothers in the murder of Sigurd. She marries Atli, leader of the Huns, but realizes that he is avaricious and desirous of obtaining Sigurd's treasure, now in the hands of Gunnar. She warns her brothers against journeying to her husband's court, using the same means found in the *Atlakvida,* the ring wound with wolf's hair. Despite Högni's advice not to go and the ill portents predicted by both Kostbera and Glaumvor, Gunnar feels that he cannot defy fate. When they are attacked at Atli's court, Gunnar and Högni are joined by Gudrun. Here, too, Högni laughs as his heart is cut out, and Gunnar plays his harp in the snake pit. Gudrun subsequently serves Atli his sons as a meal and, joined by Niblung, Högni's son, kills the Hunnish ruler in his bed. The work goes on to relate about Gudrun's attempted suicide, her marriage to King Jonakr, and the fate of her children.

## *Thidreks Saga*

Composed about the mid-thirteenth century in Norway, the *Thidreks Saga* relates the life-story of Dietrich of Bern and reflects an earlier North German source. We are told of Young Sigurd, of his apprenticeship to the smith Mimir, his fight with a dragon, and his relationship to Brünhild, from whom he receives the horse Grani. The partly demonic origin of Högni's birth is described (his father was an elf). As in Hans Sachs's *Der Hürnen Seufrid,* Sigurd and Dietrich engage each other in combat, and the hero of Bern, with the aid of his invincible sword Mimung, defeats Sigurd, who then pledges Dietrich his service. Later, Sigurd also serves as Gunnar's *Brautwerber* and tames Brünhild for the king, while receiving Grimhild as his bride. A further section deals with the murder of Sigurd at the instigation of Brünhild. Here, too, Gunnar is not portrayed as the weakling he appears to be in the *Nibelungenlied.* Not at all indecisive, he takes immediate measures when Brünhild relates the public insult done her by Grimhild (who had refused to stand in her presence and had subsequently asserted that Sigurd had robbed her of her virginity, producing her ring to prove it). Brünhild also warns Gunnar that it will not be long before they will all have to serve Sigurd. In contrast to the *Nibelungenlied,* however, Gunnar congratulates Högni for having murdered Sigurd, but Högni tries to invent excuses and is reluctant to admit to the deed. When Grimhild later maintains that Sigurd was murdered, Högni responds that he was killed by a wild boar, prompting Grimhild to accuse him of being that very animal. A section of the *Thidreks Saga* deals with "Grimhild's Revenge." In the final scenes of destruction and death, Grimhild is depicted as a she-devil who forces a torch into the mouths of her brothers Gernoz and Giselher in order to ascertain whether they are actually dead. Giselher, who had only been wounded in the preceding battle, dies as a result. Dietrich refers to Grimhild as a "she-devil," and Attila concurs with the appellation, urging Dietrich to kill his wife. Grimhild is immediately dispatched by Dietrich. The description of the extent of the catastrophe that has befallen both Niflungs (Nibelungs) and Huns in the *Thidreks Saga* is comparable to that provided by the *Nibelungenlied* poet at the conclusion of his epic.

# Appendix B:
# *Nibelungen* Prosody

In contrast to courtly romances of the period, which consist of thousands of rhyming couplets, the *Nibelungenlied* is composed in stanzas, a characteristic of heroic epics and a holdover from an earlier period when heroic songs were transmitted orally. Each stanza consists of four verses *(Langzeilen)* which are divided into rhyming pairs to give the scheme: *a a b b*. A verse is made up of two hemistichs *(Anzeile* and *Abzeile),* separated by a caesura.

Andreas Heusler's analysis of the *Nibelungen* stanza[1] has received wide critical (as well as uncritical) approval from scholars over the past fifty years. In brief, Heusler maintained that each hemistich consisted of four measures. The first hemistich of each verse also contained four stresses (the first of which could be preceded by an unaccented or opening syllable, or syllables—anacrusis, *Auftakt*). Stresses three and four occurred in the same word *(klingende Kadenz).* The second hemistich contained only three stresses, the fourth measure consisting simply of a metrical pause *(stumpfe Kadenz).* The second hemistich of the fourth verse contained a stressed syllable in the fourth measure, however, and was thus designated as "full" *(volle Kadenz).* The second measure of this hemistich is often filled by only one, long syllable, followed immediately by the accented syllable of the third measure *(beschwerte Hebung).* This emphatic conclusion to the stanza lends audible "weight" to the sense or message which the stanza is intended to convey.[2] In accordance with Heusler's theory, a *Nibelungen* stanza could be scanned as follows:

Ez wuohs in Burgonden    ein vil edel magedin
x /x́    x/ ⌒/—/ x̀ ‿// x   x /x́  x/ x́ x/x́‿/‿‿//

daz in allen landen    niht schoeners mohte sin
/x́ x/ x́ x/ ⌒ /x̀ ‿// x  /x́   x/ x́  x/ x́ ‿/‿‿//

Kriemhilt geheizen     si wart ein scoene wip
/ — /x̌ x/ — /x̌ ⸜// x /x́  x/ x́  x/ x́ ⸜/⸜⸜//

dar umbe muosen degene     vil verliesen den lip
x /x́   x/ x́  x/ —/ x̌ x// /x́  x / —/x̌ x / x́ ⸜ //

Heusler's analysis has come in for criticism of late,[3] and modern prosodists have been more inclined "to confine themselves to a purely and cautiously descriptive formula according to which hemistichs 1 to 7 contain three stresses each, the eighth 4, and 1, 3, 5, 7 as a rule have feminine and 2, 4, 6, 8 show masculine endings."[4]

The *Nibelungen* stanza may be compared to the strophic form used by the early *Minnesänger*, Der von Kürenberg (mid-twelfth century). The basic rhythmic scheme is the same, although three important differences bear noting:[5] (1) Der von Kürenberg often employs a switch in cadence (instead of "klingende Kadenz" in the first hemistich, "full" cadence, etc.). Such a switch is rare in the *Nibelungenlied*. (2) Der von Kürenberg composed his verses in "line-style," that is, the end of a sentence corresponded to the end of a verse. The *Nibelungelied* poet is more flexible, employing *enjambement*, not only between verses, but also between stanzas. (3) In contrast to Der von Kürenberg, the *Nibelungenlied* poet introduced "caesura-rhyme," although it should be noted that his use of it is occasional, that it is more frequent in manuscript C, and that its limited use in manuscript B is basically confined to the first half of the stanza.

# Notes and References

*Introduction*

1. Gottfried Weber (in association with Werner Hoffmann), *Nibelungenlied*, 3d ed., Sammlung Metzler, M 7 (Stuttgart, 1968), p. 1.

2. Hans Jacob Wagner von Wagenfels, *Ehren-Ruff Teütsch-Lands* (Vienna: Andreas Heyinger, 1692), p. 21. I am grateful to Professor Harold Jantz of Durham, North Carolina, for having first drawn my attention to this reference. In his collection of *German Baroque Literature,* it is listed as item 2610, while Curt von Faber du Faur's catalog of the collection of *German Baroque Literature* in the Yale University Library lists it as item 1514.

3. In 1557, Wolfgang Lazius of Basel had published parts of the *Nibelungenlied* in his *De gentium aliquot migrationibus.* (See Weber, *Nibelungenlied,* p. 2, n. 1.) The epic had enjoyed widespread popularity up through the thirteenth century. Of the thirty-four extant manuscripts (including fragments), the three most important are A (Hohenems-München), B (St. Gallen), and C (Hohenems-Lassberg, or Donaueschingen). The designations were established by Karl Lachmann, who considered MS A to be closest to the original version. It was MS C that Obereit discovered in 1755. Since Wilhelm Braune's construction of a manuscript stemma in 1900, most scholars have adhered to the priority accorded MS B, although the controversy that has arisen since the publication of Helmut Brackert's *Beiträge zur Handschriftenkritik des Nibelungenliedes* (Berlin, 1963), has encouraged some to consider the possibility that MS C might well be closest to the original text. See, for example, Werner Betz, "Plädoyer für C als Weg zum älteren Nibelungenlied," in *Mediaevalia litteraria: Festschrift für Helmut de Boor zum 80. Geburtstag,* ed. Ursula Hennig and Herbert Kolb (Munich, 1971), pp. 330–41. Ursula Hennig's edition of the *Nibelungenlied,* based on MS C, appeared as volume 83 of the Altdeutsche Textbibliothek in 1977.

4. Joachim Fernau, *Disteln für Hagen: Bestandsaufnahme der deutschen Seele,* 3d ed. (Munich: Herbig, 1979).

5. The original quotation reads: ". . . . Die Kenntnis dieses Gedichts gehört zu einer Bildungsstufe der Nation. . . . Jedermann sollte es lesen, damit er nach dem Mass seines Vermögens die Wirkung davon empfange" (Jubiläumsausgabe, 38: 127). These lines have been cited by at least two scholars whose approaches to the work could scarcely have been more divergent: Friedrich Panzer, *Das Nibelungenlied: Entstehung und Gestalt* (Stuttgart, 1955), and Karl Heinz Ihlenburg, *Das Nibelungenlied:*

*Problem und Gehalt* (Berlin, 1969). See Helmut Brackert's remarks in his essay "Die 'Bildungsstufe der Nation' und der Begriff der Weltliteratur: Ein Beispiel Goethescher Mittelalterrezeption," in *Goethe und die Tradition,* ed. Hans Reiss (Frankfurt: Athenäum, 1972), pp. 84–101.

6. Friedrich Heinrich von der Hagen, *Die Nibelungen: Ihre Bedeutung für die Gegenwart und für immer* (Breslau: Max, 1819); Wilhelm Müller, *Über die Lieder von den Nibelungen* (Göttingen: Vandenhoeck und Ruprecht, 1845).

7. Adolf Holtzmann, *Untersuchungen über das Nibelungenlied* (Stuttgart, 1854); Friedrich Zarncke, *Zur Nibelungenfrage* (Leipzig: S. Hirzel, 1854).

8. Karl Bartsch, *Untersuchungen über das Nibelungenlied* (Vienna, 1865).

9. Wilhelm Braune, "Die Handschriftenverhältnisse des *Nibelungenliedes,*" *PBB* 25 (1900):1–222.

10. See Weber, *Nibelungenlied,* p. 8.

11. Andreas Heusler, *Lied und Epos in germanischer Sagendichtung* (1905; reprint ed., Darmstadt: Gentner, 1956).

12. The sixth edition appeared in Dortmund in 1965 (Ruhfus) and was reprinted for the Wissenschaftliche Buchgesellschaft (Darmstadt) in 1973.

13. See Franz Rolf Schröder, "Siegfrieds Tod," *GRM* 41 (1960):111–22.

14. Ibid., particularly, p. 116.

15. Part 1 (Halle, 1941). The subsequent three volumes planned by von Kralik were never written.

16. Gustav Roethe, "Nibelungias und Waltharius," in *Sitzungsberichte der Kgl. Preuss. Akademie der Wissenschaften* (1909), pp. 649–91.

17. Karl Wilhelm Göttling, *Über das Geschichtliche im Nibelungenliede* (Rudolstadt: Verlag der Hofbuch-Handlung, 1814). The reader is directed to the concise and lucid treatment of the views of Göttling and subsequent scholars by Werner Hoffmann in *Das Siegfriedbild in der Forschung,* Erträge der Forschung, vol. 127 (Darmstadt, 1979).

18. Julius Leichtlen, *Neuaufgefundenes Bruchstück des Nibelungenliedes aus dem XIII. Jahrhundert* (Freiburg: Wagner, 1820).

19. Emil Rückert, *Oberon von Mons und die Pipine von Nivella: Untersuchungen über den Ursprung der Nibelungensage* (Leipzig: Weidmann, 1836).

20. Ludwig Ernst, *Über die Entstehung der mittelalterlichen Gedichte, welche die Deutsche Heldensage behandeln* (Rostock: Adler's Erben, 1839).

21. Georg Gottfried Gervinus, *Geschichte der deutschen Dichtung,* 5th ed. (Leipzig: Engelmann, 1871–74).

22. Gregor Sarrazin, "Der Ursprung der Siegfried-Sage," *ZfvLg,* n.s. 11 (1897):113–24.

23. A. Crüger, *Der Ursprung des Nibelungen-Liedes* (Landsberg: Volger & Klein, 1841).

24. Hermann Schneider, "Siegfried," *Forschungen und Fortschritte* 12 (1936):3–4; Theodor Frings, "Siegfried, Xanten, Niederland," *PBB* 61 (1937):364–68.

25. Georg Holz, *Der Sagenkreis der Nibelungen*, 3d ed. (Leipzig: Quelle & Meyer, 1920).

26. Gudmund Schütte, "En historisk Parallel til Nibelung-Sagnet," *ANF* 24 (1908):1–41.

27. Hugo Kuhn, "Brunhild und das Krimhidlied," in *Frühe Epik Westeuropas und die Vorgeschichte des Nibelungenliedes*, ed. Kurt Wais, vol. 1, Beihefte zur Zeitschrift für romanische Philologie, no. 95 (Tübingen: Niemeyer, 1953).

28. Helmut de Boor, "Hat Siegfried gelebt?" *PBB* 63 (1939):250–71.

29. Otto Höfler, *Siegfried, Arminius und die Symbolik: Mit einem historischen Anhang über die Varusschlacht* (Heidelberg: Winter, 1961).

30. Von der Hagen, *Die Nibelungen*, pp. 37, 137, 143.

31. Panzer, *Das Nibelungenlied*, pp. 285ff.

32. Hoffmann, *Das Siegfriedbild in der Forschung*, pp. 75–76.

33. Milman Parry's investigation of Serbocroatian heroic verse is documented by over 3,500 records and 12,500 texts which constitute the Milman Parry Collection of Harvard University. See Milman Parry, ed., *The Making of Homeric Verse: The Collected Papers of Milman Parry* (Oxford: Clarendon Press, 1971); Albert B. Lord, *The Singer of Tales* (New York: Atheneum, 1968).

34. Francis P. Magoun, Jr., "Oral-Formulaic Character of Anglo-Saxon Narrative Poetry," *Speculum* 28 (1953):446–67.

35. Franz H. Bäuml and Donald J. Ward, "Zur mündlichen Überlieferung des *Nibelungenliedes*," *DVjs* 41 (1967):351–90. Bäuml is the actual author of the article, but he graciously acknowledges his debt to Ward for some basic suggestions on the subject. See further, Bäuml, "Der Übergang mündlicher zur artes-bestimmten Literatur des Mittelalters," in *Fachliteratur des Mittelalters. Festschrift für Gerhard Eis* (Stuttgart: Metzler, 1968), pp. 1–10; Franz H. Bäuml and Agnes M. Bruno, "Weiteres zur mündlichen Überlieferung des *Nibelungenliedes*," *DVjs* 46 (1972):479–93; Franz H. Bäuml and Edda Spielmann, "From Illiteracy to Literacy: Prolegomena to a Study of the *Nibelungenlied*," *Forum for Modern Language Studies* 10 (1974):248–59; Franz H. Bäuml, "The Unmaking of the Hero: Some Critical Implications of the Transition from Oral to Written Epic," in *The Epic in Medieval Society: Aesthetic and Moral Values*, ed. Harald Scholler (Tübingen: Niemeyer, 1977), pp. 86–89.

36. See Edward R. Haymes, *Das mündliche Epos: Eine Einführung in die "Oral Poetry" Forschung,* Sammlung Metzler, M 151 (Stuttgart: Metzler, 1977). See also Haymes, "The Oral Theme of Arrival in the *Nibelungenlied,*" *CG* 3–4 (1975):159–66; Haymes, *Mündliches Epos in mittelhochdeutscher Zeit,* Göppinger Arbeiten zur Germanistik, no. 164 (Göppingen: Kümmerle, 1975). Note also Kees H. R. Borghart, *Das Nibelungenlied: Die Spuren mündlichen Ursprungs in schriftlicher Überlieferung,* Amsterdamer Publikationen zur Sprache und Literatur, vol. 31 (Amsterdam, 1977).

37. Michael Curschmann, "*Nibelungenlied* und *Nibelungenklage:* Über Mündlichkeit und Schriftlichkeit im Prozess der Episierung," in *Deutsche Literatur im Mittelalter: Kontakte und Perspektiven: Hugo Kuhn zum Gedenken,* ed. Christoph Cormeau (Stuttgart, 1979), p. 87.

38. *Das Nibelungenlied,* after the edition by Karl Bartsch, ed. Helmut de Boor, 21st ed., enlarged by Roswitha Wisniewski, Deutsche Klassiker des Mittelalters (Wiesbaden, 1979). The translations are my own. Hereafter references are cited in parentheses in the text.

39. It strikes me as a moot point to pursue the dating question any further. By this I do not mean to imply that establishing the actual date of composition is always irrelevant to the understanding of a literary work. A novel published in Germany in 1946 will be interpreted according to very different criteria (depending, of course, on the interpreter) than one published in 1942. But the general way of looking at the world did not change radically between 1198 and 1204. What is important is to have some knowledge of the culture in which the *Nibelungenlied* found the form in which it has been passed on to us, to realize that it is a product of the German High Middle Ages, an enigma at a time when Arthurian epic and *Minnesang* held sway.

40. Walter Falk, *Das Nibelungenlied in seiner Epoche: Revision eines romantischen Mythos,* Germanische Bibliothek (Heidelberg, 1974), p. 258.

*Chapter One*

1. The reader is cautioned that the translation of these four medieval terms is a complicated undertaking, and that the English expressions used are but approximations which, by their very nature, cannot convey the full semantic spectrum of the original concepts.

2. Franz Bäuml, *Medieval Civilization in Germany, 800–1273* (New York: Praeger, 1969), p. 146.

3. The term *Ritter* ("knight") must be used cautiously, as Joachim Bumke has shown in his illuminating monograph, *Studien zum Ritterbegriff im 12. und 13. Jahrhundert,* Beihefte zum *Euphorion,* vol. 1 (Heidelberg: Carl Winter, 1964). The concept was employed during the Middle High German *Blütezeit* as a designation for a soldier of lower social standing as well as for the nobility. (See Bumke, pp. 35–59.) In our discussion, the

"knight" is understood to be a member of the upper class, directly below the king on the social scale. He normally held his lands in vassalage from the king or received them in payment for his service. He is, in the words of Bumke (p. 88), "der adlige Ritter" ("the noble knight").

4. Note, for example, Hartmann von Aue, *Der arme Heinrich,* vv. 12–15, Walther von der Vogelweide, "Ich saz ûf eime steine," vv. 9–22, and Wolfram von Eschenbach, *Parzival,* block 827, vv. 19–24.

5. See Gustav Ehrismann, "Die Grundlagen des ritterlichen Tugendsystems," *ZfdA* 56 (1919):137–216; Ernst Robert Curtius, "Das ritterliche Tugendsystem," *DVjs* 21 (1943):343–68; Friedrich Maurer, "Das ritterliche Tugendsystem," in *Dichtung und Sprache des Mittelalters: Gesammelte Aufsätze* (Bern: Francke, 1963), pp. 23–37.

6. Erich Auerbach, *Mimesis: The Representation of Reality in Western Literature,* trans. Willard R. Trask (Princeton: Princeton University Press, 1968), pp. 136–37.

7. Morris Bishop, *The Middle Ages* (New York: American Heritage Press, 1970), p. 129.

8. Clement C. J. Webb, ed., *Ioannis Saresberiensis Episcopi Carnotensis Policratici sive De Nugis Curialium et Vestigiis Philosophorum Libre VIII* (Oxford: Clarendon Press, 1909), vol. 2, bk. 6.

9. Eileen Power, *Medieval Women,* ed. M. M. Postan (Cambridge: Cambridge University Press, 1976), p. 12.

10. Karl Heinz Ihlenburg regards the epic as an "expression of the feudal-courtly period around 1200" (*Das Nibelungenlied,* p. 35). His commentary on "Feudalhöfische Dichtung und feudale Ideologie" (pp. 35–41) contrasts the "ideal world of courtly poetry" (p. 40) with feudal reality. In essence, the chivalrous ideal of virtue remained a dream.

11. Joachim Bumke, *Mäzene im Mittelalter: Die Gönner und Auftraggeber der höfischen Literatur in Deutschland 1150–1300* (Munich, 1979), p. 9.

12. See, for example, Helmut de Boor, ed., *Das Nibelungenlied,* pp. vii–viii.

13. Andreas Heusler, *Nibelungensage und Nibelungenlied,* 6th ed. (Dortmund, 1965), p. 44.

14. Willy Krogmann, *Der Dichter des Nibelungenliedes,* Philologische Studien und Quellen, vol. 11 (Berlin: Erich Schmidt, 1962).

15. George F. Jones, "ze Osterrich lernt ich singen unde sagen (Walther 32, 14)," *Leuvensche Bijdragen* 58 (1969):77.

16. Berta Lösel-Wieland-Engelmann, "Verdanken wir das Nibelungenlied einer Niedernburger Nonne?" *Monatshefte* 72 (1980):5–25.

17. Bumke, *Mäzene im Mittelalter,* p. 71.

18. See Hugo Bekker, *The Nibelungenlied: A Literary Analysis* (Toronto, 1971); Nelly Dürrenmatt, *Das Nibelungenlied im Kreis der höfischen Dichtung* (Bern, 1945).

19. See Bert Nagel, *Das Nibelungenlied: Stoff—Form—Ethos* (Frankfurt, 1965), p. 269: "[T]he poet is not the critic of a specific ideology, but rather a *tragic poet* who, in the broadest sense of the word, suffers under the imperfection of human existence." Ihlenburg, *Das Nibelungenlied,* p. 41, points to the dichotomy between the harmonious conclusion of the Arthurian romance and the "tragic concept of the *Nibelungenlied* poet."

*Chapter Two*

1. Gottfried Weber, *Das Nibelungenlied: Problem und Idee* (Stuttgart, 1963), p. 6.

2. Friedrich Maurer, *Leid: Studien zur Bedeutungs- und Problemgeschichte, besonders in den grossen Epen der staufischen Zeit* (Bern, 1969), p. 19.

3. A. T. Hatto, trans., *The Nibelungenlied* (New York, 1976), p. 112, n. 3.

4. Note also 898.2 ("mit triuwen," "in loyalty"), 901.1 ("vil lieber vriunt," "my dear friend"), and 901.2 ("dîne triuwe," "your loyalty"). "Vriunt" may actually convey more than the idea of "friend" in this context, as Kriemhild maintains in 898.1 that Hagen is her "mâc" (that is, "relative") as she is his.

5. I regard the references to the church and mass, as well as to God, in the *Nibelungenlied* to be purely formal. A case might be made for Rüdeger's "deeper" Christianity, but this, as we shall see, is also open to dispute.

6. Werner Schröder, "Zum Problem der Hortfrage im Nibelungenlied," in *Nibelungenlied-Studien* (Stuttgart: Metzler, 1968), pp. 157–84.

7. While Kriemhild is portrayed as a calculating schemer at this point, it is noteworthy that the poet refers to her, not without respect, as "diu getriuwe" ("that loyal woman," 1259.1).

8. Ihlenburg, *Das Nibelungenlied,* p. 85.

9. De Boor, ed., *Das Nibelungenlied,* p. 276, commentary to 1748.4.

10. Werner Hoffmann, *Das Nibelungenlied;* Interpretationen zum Deutschunterricht (Munich, 1969), pp. 66–67.

11. Unlike the author of *Diu Klage* (see chapter 5), who admires Kriemhild's long-standing loyalty toward her dead husband.

12. Hoffmann, *Das Nibelungenlied.* p. 73.

13. The allusion to the death of Kriemhild's future spouse contained within the first *Aventiure* is scarcely forgotten when we meet Siegfried. Only the dullest members of the poet's audience could fail to form some conjecture concerning the potential relationship between Kriemhild and

Siegfried and to conclude that the harmony which prevails in Xanten furnishes a stark contrast to what has been predicted for Worms!

14. Siegfried seems concerned about "legitimizing" himself as future king of Xanten. He is not as eager to inherit land from his father as he is to win it in battle (see 109.3). Whether he defies the *ordo* of society in the process is of no concern to him. In this respect, he has something in common with young Parzival, whose self-centeredness as a youth creates disorder in the world about him.

15. Weber, *Das Nibelungenlied: Problem und Idee,* p. 22.

16. See Theodore M. Andersson, *The Legend of Brynhild* (Ithaca, 1980), in particular, p. 69, "Summary."

17. "Demonic" in the sense that it allows Siegfried to disregard the more natural affinity between himself and Brünhild. The reader will recall the association between Kriemhild's beauty and death emphasized already in 2.3–4.

18. Most recently by Theodore M. Andersson, "Why does Siegfried die?" in *Germanic Studies in Honor of Otto Springer,* ed. Stephen J. Kaplowitt (Pittsburgh, 1978), pp. 29–39. Andersson surveys the responses of scholars to this question between 1960 and 1970. He rejects all of the theories based on a textual analysis which does not consider the tradition and concludes: "In the final analysis, the reason for Siegfried's death cannot be found in the actions or the passions of the characters, but only in the tradition. The poet removed the breach of faith in his source and devised nothing adequate with which to replace it. In the *Nibelungenlied* Siegfried dies for no good reason at all" (p. 38). In his article, "Die Darstellung von Siegfrieds Tod und die Entwicklung des Hagenbildes in der Nibelungendichtung" (*GRM,* n.s. 21 (1971):369–78), Helmut K. Krausse refers to the vagueness of the motivation for Siegfried's death in the *Nibelungenlied* (p. 370). We may take issue, however, with Krausse's later statement that Siegfried, at the stream, is the "epitome of the courtly knight" (p. 373).

19. Weber, *Das Nibelungenlied: Problem und Idee,* pp. 56–58; see also Gerd Backenköhler, *Untersuchungen zur Gestalt Hagens von Tronje in den mittelalterlichen Nibelungendichtungen* (Bonn, 1961).

20. See Francis G. Gentry, "Hagen and the Problem of Individuality in the *Nibelungenlied,*" *Monatshefte* 68 (1976):7.

21. See below, Appendix A (allusion to Högni's, that is, Hagen's, supernatural father in the *Thidreks Saga*).

22. D. G. Mowatt and Hugh Sacker, *The Nibelungenlied: An Interpretative Commentary* (Toronto, 1967), p. 132, commentary to 2012.1.

23. Ibid.

24. While the numerous references to the treacherous nature of Hagen's act (see above, p. 34) would support this statement, it could be

argued that once time had had a chance to "relativize" the murder, the killing of Siegfried may have brought Hagen more fame than notoriety (note 1733).

25. See, however, the article by H. B. Willson, "Blood and Wounds in the 'Nibelungenlied' " *MLR* 55 (1960):40–50, in particular, pp. 42–43. In "*Ordo* and *Inordinatio* in the Nibelungenlied" (*PBB* 85 (1963):341), Willson states that "the scene is a *Gegenbild* of the Eucharist." See also "Echoes of St. Paul in the *Nibelungenlied*," *MLN* 84, no. 5 (1969):699–715, in particular, pp. 713–14. There is no reason to believe that the blood-drinking scene in the Great Hall is an antithetical analogy (at least, not an intended one) to the Eucharist, as Willson maintains. See Werner Hoffmann's critical remarks on H. B. Willson's theses in *Kudrun: Ein Beitrag zur Deutung der nachnibelungischen Heldendichtung,* Germanistische Abhandlungen, vol. 17 (Stuttgart: Metzler, 1967), pp. 245–49.

26. Gottfried Weber declares hubris to be integral to heroic comportment. See *Das Nibelungenlied: Problem und Idee,* p. 57.

27. Ibid., p. 56.

28. Weber makes a clear distinction, however, between the coarse, Nordic beauty of Brünhild and the more refined features of the Rhenish Kriemhild (ibid., p. 35).

29. Andersson, *The Legend of Brynhild,* p. 243.


*Chapter Three*

1. Weber, *Das Nibelungenlied,* p. 69.

2. See L. C. Wrenn, ed., *Beowulf with the Finnesburg Fragment* (London: Harrap, 1973), vv. 1687ff., in particular, vv. 1760–61: "ofer-hȳda ne gȳm,/mǣre cempa" ("Avoid pride, illustrious warrior").

3. Weber, *Das Nibelungenlied,* p. 83.

4. Bert Nagel has referred to Rüdeger as the personification of Christian chivalry: "Heidnisches und Christliches im Nibelungenlied," *Ruperto-Carola* 24 (1958):61ff. See also R. G. Finch, "Rüdiger and Dietrich," *Trivium* 12 (1977):39–57. The most comprehensive treatment of Rüdeger to date is Jochen Splett's *Rüdiger von Bechelaren: Studien zum zweiten Teil des Nibelungenliedes* (Heidelberg: Winter, 1968).

5. Nagel, *Das Nibelungenlied,* p. 11.

6. Bert Nagel, "Das Dietrichbild des Nibelungenliedes," *ZfdPh* 78 (1959):262.

7. Ibid.

8. See Blanka Horacek, "Der Charakter Dietrichs von Bern im *Nibelungenlied*," in *Festgabe für Otto Höfler zum 70. Geburtstag,* ed. Helmut Birkhan, Philologica Germanica, no. 3 (Stuttgart: Braumüller, 1976). Horacek takes issue with the prevailing positive portrayal of Dietrich and cites textual evidence to demonstrate the hero's basic egocentricity.

9. See Finch, "Rüdiger and Dietrich," p. 55.

10. Note Weber, *Das Nibelungenlied,* p. 170, and Nagel, *Das Nibelungenlied,* p. 265.

11. Friedrich Panzer, *Studien zum Nibelungenliede* (Frankfurt, 1945), p. 95. See also Splett, *Rüdiger von Bechelaren,* p. 46 and passim.

12. See Weber, *Das Nibelungenlied,* p. 207; Ihlenburg, *Das Nibelungenlied,* p. 117.

13. Note George Fenwick Jones, "Rüdiger's Dilemma," *Studies in Philology* 57 (1960): 19: "[Rüdiger] seems to believe that God damns those who violate their promise of safe-conduct [2150.3–4], although it was the heathen Teutons rather than the Christians who scorned this practice. In spite of this much-mentioned concern for his soul, Rüdiger nevertheless decides in favor of his worldly reputation and shows that, even in his case, pagan values outweighed Christian ones."

14. Note also 2156.4. Rüdeger's assertion in 2160 that people could easily gain the impression he had turned coward also indicates the knight's concern with his worldly image.

15. See, however, Peter Wapnewski, "Rüdigers Schild," *Euphorion* 54 (1960):380–410. Wapnewski rejects religion as a basis for Rüdeger's conflict, claiming that it is, in essence, a legal matter.

16. Hermann Schneider, *Heldendichtung, Geistlichendichtung, Ritterdichtung* (Heidelberg: Winter, 1925), p. 372; see also Hans Naumann, "Rüdigers Tod," *DVjs* 10 (1932):402.

17. Mowatt and Sacker, *The Nibelungenlied,* p. 139, commentary to 2196–97.

18. In "Die Einheit des Nibelungenlieds nach Idee und Form," *DU* 5 (1953):36, Friedrich Maurer claims that "Rüdeger acts neither as a Christian nor as a courtly knight, but rather as a Germanic hero. He has strayed from both God and his *ordo.* The decision he takes is completely unChristian, God-less, and thus he is not saved by divine grace but rather fulfills his fate. . . . No God intervenes to provide him with assistance; there is only death, which either ends or prevents dishonor and sorrow."

19. Weber, *Das Nibelungenlied,* p. 66.

*Chapter Four*

1. H. Timm, *Das Nibelungenlied: Nach Darstellung und Sprache ein Urbild deutscher Poesie* (Halle: Schroedel & Simon, 1852), p. 40.

2. See Hans J. Bayer, *Untersuchungen zum Sprachstil weltlicher Epen des deutschen Früh- und Hochmittelalters,* Philologische Studien und Quellen, vol. 10 (Berlin: Erich Schmidt, 1962), p. 5.

3. Bert Nagel, *Staufische Klassik: Deutsche Dichtung um 1200* (Heidelberg: Lothar Stiehm, 1977), p. 502.

4. Ibid., p. 503.

5. See Dürrenmatt, *Das Nibelungenlied im Kreis der höfischen Dichtung,* and Walter Johannes Schröder, "Das Nibelungenlied," *PBB* 76 (1954–55):56–143.

6. See Georg Radke, *Die epische Formel im Nibelungenliede* (Fraustadt: Pucher, 1890), p. 6, and Bayer, *Untersuchungen zum Sprachstil weltlicher Epen,* pp. 17ff. Bayer compared 1,000 verses in heroic epics and courtly romances and determined that while the *Nibelungenlied* evinced a ratio of 260 abstract concepts to 650 concrete terms (*Kudrun* 245 to 605), Hartmann von Aue's *Iwein* produced 395 abstract to 350 concrete.

7. The presence of such precourtly (or uncourtly) elements in the *Nibelungenlied* is not advanced as the principal criterion for its classification as an "heroic epic." Hugo Kuhn has considered the difficulties of such an undertaking in "Gattungsprobleme der mittelhochdeutschen Literatur," in *Dichtung und Welt im Mittelalter,* 2d ed. (Stuttgart: Metzler, 1969), pp. 41–61. I tend to agree with Lascelles Abercrombie that "[r]igid definitions in literature are . . . dangerous. At bottom, it is what we feel, not what we think, that makes us put certain poems together and apart from others" (*The Epic: an Essay* [London: Martin Secker, 1922], p. 50).

8. Bayer, *Untersuchungen zum Sprachstil weltlicher Epen,* p. 80.

9. A fine combing of the text will turn up examples of apokoinu, litotes, monologue, the rare allegory, personification, asyndeton, and synecdoche. The poet is not without a sense of humor (note 649f., and 959). The repetition of stock phrases (epic formulas), appellatives, and epithets is particularly characteristic. While more archaic forms abound in the lexical sphere, one of the most prominent traits of Germanic poetry, alliterative verse, occurs relatively seldom in the *Nibelungenlied.* See Otto Vilmar, "Reste der Alliteration im Nibelungenliede," in *Programm des Kurfürstlichen Gymnasiums zu Hanau* (Hanau: Waisenhaus-Buchdruckerei, 1855), pp. 1–36.

10. Panzer, *Das Nibelungenlied,* p. 134.

11. Compare and contrast 2009.3, where the epithet is applied most fittingly to Volker and Hagen.

12. Timm, *Das Nibelungenlied,* p. 101.

13. Mowatt and Sacker, *The Nibelungenlied,* p. 92, commentary to 976.2–3.

14. Concerning symbolism and the intention of a writer, see Rudolph von Abele, "Symbolism and the Student," *College English* 16 (1955):424–29, particularly pp. 428–29, and Walter Havighurst, "Symbolism and the Student," *College English* 16 (1955):429–34, 461, especially pp. 429–30. Excerpts from both contributions are reprinted in *Literary Symbolism: An Introduction to the Interpretation of Literature,* ed. Maurice Beebe (San Francisco: Wadsworth, 1960), pp. 14–15.

15. Timm, *Das Nibelungenlied,* pp. 75, 77.

16. It is for this reason that one will find it difficult to concur with Werner A. Mueller that the *Nibelungenlied,* "[a]s work of art, projecting man into infinity . . . symbolizes faith, admitting man's potential of spirituality, yet leaving God, His power and His will subject to individual experience, to individual search" (*The Nibelungenlied Today: Its Substance, Essence, and Significance,* University of North Carolina Studies in the Germanic Languages and Literatures, no. 34 [Chapel Hill: University of North Carolina Press, 1962], p. 92).

17. Hansjürgen Linke, "Über den Erzähler im Nibelungenlied und seine künstlerische Funktion," *GRM* 41 (1960):377.

18. Ibid.

19. Linke claims that the poet needed to explain to his public how Kriemhild could break her pact of reconciliation with her brother. He sees the narrator functioning here as a middleman between archaic heroic subject matter and a courtly public. ("Über den Erzähler im Nibelungenlied," p. 378.)

20. Panzer, *Das Nibelungenlied,* p. 171.

21. See Siegfried Beyschlag, "Die Funktion der epischen Vorausdeutung im Aufbau des Nibelungenlieds," *PBB* 76 (Halle, 1954–55):38–55. Note also Burghart Wachinger, *Studien zum Nibelungenlied: Vorausdeutungen, Aufbau, Motivierung* (Tübingen: Niemeyer, 1960).

22. Panzer, *Das Nibelungenlied,* p. 120.

23. Hatto contends that "hints of what will happen remain dark. Never is the future made so precise as to detract from the immediacy of the present" (*The Nibelungenlied,* p. 311).

24. Panzer, *Das Nibelungenlied,* p. 120: "The essential thing is that, through these predictions, the entire epic has been given an air of melancholy, so to speak; the whole work seems to be saturated by 'an atmosphere of impending fate.' "

25. Such reminders of what is to transpire were undoubtedly very effective, perhaps even necessary, in holding the interest of the public when the tale was recited orally.

26. De Boor, ed., *Das Nibelungenlied,* p. xviii.

27. See the various possibilities cited by Peter Wiehl in his article, "Über den Aufbau des Nibelungenliedes," *WW* 16 (1966):309–23. Several criteria suggest themselves for a structural analysis of the *Nibelungenlied:* time, journeys, key concepts, as well as numerical symmetry.

28. De Boor, ed., *Das Nibelungenlied,* p. xx, and Burghart Wachinger, *Studien zum Nibelungenlied,* pp. 56, 100.

29. De Boor, ed., *Das Nibelungenlied,* p. xix.

30. For a lucid analysis of the function of *leit* both within the *Nibelungenlied* and various other works of the Middle High German *Blütezeit,*

see Friedrich Maurer, *Leid: Studien zur Bedeutungs- und Problemgeschichte, besonders in den grossen Epen der staufischen Zeit.*

31. Hatto, trans., *The Nibelungenlied,* pp. 301–12.

*Chapter Five*

1. Holger Schulz, *Der Nibelungenstoff auf dem deutschen Theater* (Cologne: F. Hansen, 1972).

2. Otfrid Ehrismann, *Das Nibelungenlied in Deutschland: Studien zur Rezeption des Nibelungenlieds von der Mitte des 18. Jahrhunderts bis zum Ersten Weltkrieg,* Münchner Universitäts-Schriften, Philosophische Fakultät, vol. 14 (Munich, 1975).

3. Werner Wunderlich, ed., *Der Schatz des Drachentödters: Materialien zur Wirkungsgeschichte des Nibelungenliedes,* Literaturwissenschaft, Gesellschaftswissenschaft, no. 30 (Stuttgart, 1977).

4. Henry and Mary Garland, *The Oxford Companion to German Literature* (Oxford: Clarendon Press, 1976), p. 635, s.v. *Nibelungenlied.*

5. *Diu Klage: Mit den Lesarten sämtlicher Handschriften,* ed. Karl Bartsch (1875; reprint ed., Darmstadt, 1964). Quotations in my text are based on this edition.

6. Despite his words in praise of Kriemhild's *triuwe,* it is difficult to imagine how the *Klage* poet could possibly have felt a reconciliation possible between the queen's obsession with revenge and her absolutism on the one hand, and Christian principles on the other.

7. K. C. King, ed., *Das Lied vom Hürnen Seyfrid,* with introduction and notes (Manchester: University of Manchester Press, 1958). Quotations in my text are based on this edition.

8. It should be noted that while in the *Lied* Seyfrid dies in a forest, this is not the case in the *Nibelungenlied.* The murder takes place by a stream in a grove on the periphery of the forest. Common to both works is Siegfried's tendency to be overbearing, a source of *sorge,* and hence *leit,* to those around him.

9. Wilhelm Grimm, *Die deutsche Heldensage,* 4th ed. (1889; reprint ed., Darmstadt: Wissenschaftliche Buchgesellschaft, 1957), p. 284.

10. King, ed., *Das Lied vom Hürnen Seyfrid,* p. 40.

11. Hans Sachs, *Der Hürnen Seufrid: Tragoedie in sieben Acten,* ed. Edmund Goetze, 2d ed., Neudrucke deutscher Literaturwerke, Neue Folge, vol. 19 (Tübingen: Niemeyer, 1967), act 1, verse 56.

12. Ibid., act 1, verse 58.

13. An excellent review of the reception of *Der Hürnen Seyfrid* (as well as heroic themes in general) in sixteenth-century Nuremberg is provided by Helmut Weinacht, "Das Motiv vom Hürnen Seyfrid im Nürnberg des 16. Jahrhunderts: Zum Problem der bürgerlichen Rezeption heldenepischer Stoffe," in *Hans Sachs und Nürnberg: Bedingungen und Probleme*

*reichsstädtischer Literatur: Hans Sachs zum 400. Todestag am 19. Januar 1976,* ed. Horst Brunner, Gerhard Hirschmann, and Fritz Schnelbögl, Nürnberger Forschungen, vol. 19 (Nuremberg: Selbstverein des Verlags für Geschichte, 1976), pp. 137–81.

14. See, for example, Henry and Mary Garland, *The Oxford Companion to German Literature,* p. 412, s.v. *Hürnen Seyfrid, Der.* Weinacht, however, acknowledges the fact that 1726 is simply the date of the latest extant edition, and refers to the article by Jantz noted below in n. 15.

15. Harold Jantz, "The Last Branch of the Nibelungen Tree," *MLN* 80 (1965):433–40.

16. Scholars had long assumed that this was probably an allusion to a fictitious tale, but the work did, in fact, exist, and a copy of it may be found in the Harold Jantz Collection at Duke University.

17. See the selection provided by Werner Wunderlich in *Der Schatz des Drachentödters,* p. 21.

18. See above, n. 1. This is the best survey in print of dramatizations of the *Nibelungenlied* on the German stage during the nineteenth and twentieth centuries.

19. Werner Wunderlich lists a total of thirty-three dramatic productions between 1821 and 1918. It is worth noting that the first attempt since Hans Sachs to dramatize the *Nibelungen* theme, the trilogy, *Der Held des Nordens* (The hero of the north), by Friedrich Baron de la Motte Fouqué (dedicated to J. G. Fichte), is based on the Eddic lays and the first two parts of the *Völsunga Saga,* as well as the *Ragnar Saga.*

20. For a discussion of thirty-four performances of Hebbel's *Nibelungen* (or individual parts of the trilogy) between 31 January 1861, when it premiered at the Grossherzogliches Hoftheater in Weimar, and 21 May 1925, see Walther Landgrebe, *Hebbels Dichtungen auf der Bühne,* Forschungen zur Literatur-, Theater- und Zeitungswissenschaft, vol. 1 (Oldenburg: Schulz, 1927).

21. Schulz, *Der Nibelungenstoff auf dem deutschen Theater,* p. 95.

22. Weber, *Nibelungenlied,* p. 88.

23. Friedrich Rückert, "Sigurd unter den Gänsen," in *Friedrich Rükkerts gesammelte Poetische Werke,* vol. 7 (Frankfurt am Main: Sauerländer, 1868), p. 57.

24. In this regard, note the letter written to Hebbel by Georg Gottfried Gervinus in which the latter stated: "I have always considered it something of an impossibility to bring the figures of the old epics onto the stage" (Friedrich Hebbel, *Sämtliche Werke,* ed. Richard Maria Weber, vol. 7, *Briefe,* appendix [Berlin: B. Behr, 1901–7], p. 410).

25. Friedrich Hebbel, "An den geneigten Leser," posthumously published foreword to the *Nibelungen,* in *Hebbels Werke,* ed. Theodor Poppe (Berlin: Bong & Co., 1923), 5:12. A fine introduction to Hebbel's *Ni-*

*belungen* is offered by Sten G. Flygt, *Friedrich Hebbel,* Twayne's World Authors Series, no. 56 (New York: Twayne Publishers, 1968), pp. 132–41. Note also Wilhelm Emrich, *Hebbels Nibelungen: Götzen und Götter der Moderne,* Akademie der Wissenschaften und der Literatur, Jahrgang 1973–74, no. 6 (Mainz: Akademie der Wissenschaften und der Literatur, 1974).

26. See Schulz, *Der Nibelungenstoff auf dem deutschen Theater,* p. 84.

27. Friedrich Hebbel, *Die Nibelungen,* in *Hebbels Werke in zwei Bänden,* ed. Walther Vontin, vol. 2, *Dramen und Prosa* (Hamburg: Hoffmann and Campe Verlag, n.d.), pp. 14–15 (*Vorspiel,* scene 2).

28. Ibid., p. 28 (*Vorspiel,* scene 4). Quotes in text are based on the Vontin edition.

29. Ibid., p. 203.

30. See Jost Hermand, "Hebbels '*Nibelungen*'—Ein deutsches Trauerspiel," in *Hebbel in neuer Sicht,* ed. Helmut Kreuzer, 2d ed., Sprache und Literatur, vol. 9 (Stuttgart: Kohlhammer, 1969), p. 330. See, however, Sten G. Flygt, *Friedrich Hebbel,* p. 134: "The inexorable duty to exact vengeance is, of course, the feature of heathendom which brings about its collapse. The chaplain, Rüdeger, and Dietrich von Bern represent the new form of the Idea, Christianity, with its ethical norms of self-control, humility, and readiness to forgive."

31. Quoted by Raymond Mander and Joe Mitchenson, *The Wagner Companion* (New York: Hawthorn Books, 1977), p. 159.

32. Wunderlich, *Der Schatz des Drachentödters,* p. 51.

33. Ernst Alker, *Die deutsche Literatur im 19. Jahrhundert* (Stuttgart: A. Kröner, 1961), p. 734.

34. Paul Ernst, "Nachwort zu Chriemhild," in *Gesammelte Dramen,* vol. 2, pt. 1 (Munich: Georg Müller, 1922), p. 325. It is worth noting that Ernst considered Hagen to be the "personification of the idea of the German people" (p. 324).

35. See Karl Hunger, "Paul Ernsts 'Brunhild' and 'Chriemhild,' " *Zeitschrift für deutsche Bildung* 2 (1941):33.

36. Paul Ernst, "Die Nibelungen: Stoff, Epos und Drama," in *Weg zur Form,* 3d ed. (Munich: G. Müller, 1928), p. 171.

37. Note Ernst, *Brunhild: Trauerspiel in drei Aufzügen,* in *Gesammelte Dramen,* vol. 2, pt. 1 (Munich: Georg Müller, 1922), act 1 (p. 203):

> "Ihr zwei seid das Geschwür in unserm Leib,
> Und Selbstvernichtungswut ist euer Leben.
> .........................................
> Wär' ich dein Mann nicht: dich wollt' ich ermorden,
> Chriemhild und dich. Dann wäre alles gut."

("You two are the cancer in our body and you are possessed by a death-wish. If I were not your vassal, I would kill both you and Kriemhild. Then everything would be fine.")

38. See, for example, Adolf Hitler, *Mein Kampf*, 72d ed. (Munich: Franz Eher, 1933), p. 707: "the struggling Siegfried fell victim to the stab in the back."

39. Werner Wunderlich, *Der Schatz des Drachentödters*, p. 86.

40. This attempt to acknowledge positive attributes in Hagen some-times led to contradictions among authors of the period as to how, pre-cisely, the figure ought to be interpreted. Wilhelm Helmich, for example, referred to the manner in which children loved the "fairy-tale hero" Sieg-fried, and hated his antagonist, Hagen ("Deutsch," in Ernst Dobbers and Kurt Higelke, eds., *Rassenpolitische Unterrichtspraxis: Der Rassengedanke in der Unterrichtsgestaltung der Volksschulfächer* [Leipzig: Julius Klinkhardt, 1939], p. 34). Note, on the other hand, the positive portrayal of Hagen at the conclusion of Friedrich Schreyvogel's novel, *Die Nibelungen* (1940).

41. Wunderlich, *Der Schatz des Drachentödters*, p. 90.

42. The last division formed in the Waffen-SS (Combat SS) in March and April 1945, consisting in large part of recruits from the SS-Junker-schule (SS Officer Training School) at Bad Tölz, was the 38th SS-Panzer Grenadier Division, designated "Nibelungen." The heavily fortified de-fense network built along the French-German border between 1933 and 1938 was known as both the *Westwall* and the *Siegfriedlinie*.

43. Note Wunderlich, *Der Schatz des Drachentödters*, p. 97.

44. However, a considerable number of translations of the *Nibelungen-lied* into New High German have appeared from the late fifties through to the seventies, including those of Helmut de Boor (1959), Felix Genzmer (1961), Horst Wolfram Geissler (1966), Helmut Brackert (1970), and Ulrich Pretzel (1973).

45. "Neu erzählen—neu gewinnen," Arbeitsgespräch mit Franz Fühmann, in *Neue deutsche Literatur* 18, no. 2 (1970):68.

46. Werner Wunderlich, *Der Schatz des Drachentödters*, p. 118. Schaumburg's earlier remarks on the subject should be noted: "Etzels Ende," *Der Spiegel* 29, no. 40 (1975):222–25. The suggestion that Soest may have actually been the "location" of the Nibelungs' demise is not new. See ten Doornkaat Koolmann, *Soest, die Stätte des Nibelungenunter-ganges?* (Soest: Rocholsche Buchdruckerei W. Jahn, 1935).

*Chapter Six*

1. Hoffmann, *Das Siegfriedbild in der Forschung*, p. 118.

2. Bodo Mergell, "*Nibelungenlied* und höfischer Roman," *Euphorion* 45 (1950):321, refers to "a mutual assimilation and intertwining of the heroic and the religious," but I detect no overt intention on the part of

the poet to emphasize such a combination. From a theological point of view, the heroic and the religious (i.e. heathen heroism and Christianity) are, indeed, mutually exclusive. I would agree with Nagel that "they can only be portrayed as existing simultaneously and in contrast to each other, but not assimilated" (*Das Nibelungenlied,* p. 206).

3. Nagel, *Das Nibelungenlied,* p. 205.

4. See Werner Schröder, "Die Tragödie Kriemhilts im Nibelungenlied," *ZfdA* 90 (1960–61):45; Werner Hoffmann, *Kudrun: Ein Beitrag zur Deutung der nachnibelungischen Heldendichtung,* Germanistische Abhandlungen, vol. 17 (Stuttgart: Metzler, 1967), pp. 20–21; Nagel, *Staufische Klassik,* pp. 456, 462, and passim.

5. See Hatto's concise summary of some of the epic's shortcomings under this subtitle in his translation of the *Nibelungenlied,* pp. 301–12.

6. Ibid., p. 347.

7. Ibid.

8. Nagel, *Das Nibelungenlied,* p. 271.

9. Ibid.

*Appendix A*

1. In the following pages, I have only given consideration to the *Poetic Edda,* not to the *Prose Edda* (Codex Wormianus) of Snorri Sturluson (1178–1241).

2. *Brot af Sigurparkvidu,* in *The Poetic Edda,* trans., with introduction and explanatory notes, by Lee M. Hollander, 2d ed. (Austin: University of Texas Press, 1962), p. 244, st. 5.

3. Hollander, *The Poetic Edda,* p. 294.

*Appendix B*

1. See Andreas Heusler, *Deutsche Versgeschichte,* vol. 2, pt. 3, *Der altdeutsche Vers,* 2d ed., Grundriss der Germanischen Philologie (Berlin: Walter de Gruyter & Co., 1956), in particular, pp. 253ff.

2. See Gerard Jan Hendrik Kulsdom, *Die Strophenschlüsse im Nibelungenlied: Ein Versuch,* Amsterdamer Publikationen zur Sprache und Literatur, vol. 37 (Amsterdam: Rudopi, 1979). See also, Beyschlag, "Die Funktion der epischen Vorausdeutung im Aufbau des Nibelungenliedes," pp. 38–55.

3. Note Ray M. Wakefield, *Nibelungen Prosody,* De Proprietatibus Litterarum, Series Practica, vol. 112 (The Hague: Mouton, 1976). Wakefield's approach owes much to "the theoretical assumptions and methodology of the Russian Formalists, that is, their view of meter as an abstract pattern and their sense that the task of the prosodist lies in a description of the relation of the language material to that abstract pattern" (p. 2).

4. Ulrich K. Goldsmith, "Nibelungen Stanza," *Princeton Encyclopedia of Poetry and Poetics,* ed. Alex Preminger et al., enl. ed. (Princeton: Princeton University Press, 1974), p. 570.

5. What follows is, in essence, a summary of the salient points on the subject treated by Gottfried Weber in *Nibelungenlied,* pp. 73–75.

# Selected Bibliography

## PRIMARY SOURCES

1. Editions of the *Nibelungenlied* and *Klage*

Bartsch, Karl, ed. *Diu Klage: Mit den Lesarten sämtlicher Handschriften.* 1875. Reprint. Darmstadt: Wissenschaftliche Buchgesellschaft, 1964.

Batts, Michael S., ed. *Das Nibelungenlied: Paralleldruck der Handschriften A, B und C nebst Lesarten der übrigen Handschriften.* Tübingen: Niemeyer, 1971.

De Boor, Helmut, ed. *Das Nibelungenlied.* After the edition by Karl Bartsch. 21st ed., revised and augmented by Roswitha Wisniewski. Deutsche Klassiker des Mittelalters. Wiesbaden: Brockhaus, 1979.

Engels, Heinz, ed. *Das Nibelungenlied: A Complete Transcription in Modern German Type of the Text of Manuscript C from the Fürstenberg Court Library Donaueschingen.* With an essay on the manuscript and its provenance by Erna Huber. New York: Praeger, 1969.

Hennig, Ursula, ed. *Das Nibelungenlied nach der Handschrift C.* Altdeutsche Textbibliothek, no. 83. Tübingen: Niemeyer, 1977.

2. English Translations

Hatto, A. T., trans. *The Nibelungenlied.* 1965. Reprint. Baltimore: Penguin, 1981.

Mowatt, D. G., trans. *The Nibelungenlied.* London: Dent; New York: Dutton, 1965.


## SECONDARY SOURCES

1. Bibliographies

Abeling, Theodor. *Das Nibelungenlied und seine Literatur: Eine Bibliographie und vier Abhandlungen.* 1907. Reprint. New York: B. Franklin, 1970. For older titles.

Krogmann, Willy, and Pretzel, Ulrich. *Bibliographie zum Nibelungenlied und zur Klage.* 4th ed. Berlin: Erich Schmidt, 1966.

Weber, Gottfried, together with Werner Hoffman. *Nibelungenlied*. 4th ed. Sammlung Metzler, M 7. Stuttgart: Metzler, 1974.

2. Books and Articles

Andersson, Theodore M. *The Legend of Brynhild*. Ithaca: Cornell University Press, 1980. A comprehensive survey of the role of Brünhild in the Scandinavian and German texts with two chapters devoted to the sources and composition of the *Nibelungenlied*. Heusler's approach is reaffirmed.

————. "Why does Siegried die?" In *Germanic Studies in Honor of Otto Springer,* edited by Stephen J. Kaplowitt. Pittsburgh: K & S Enterprises, 1978, pp. 29–39. Andersson maintains that Siegfried's death in the *Nibelungenlied* can only be understood if the tradition is taken into account.

Bartsch, Karl. *Untersuchungen über das Nibelungenlied*. Vienna: Braumüller, 1865. Dated but helpful study by one of the greatest *Nibelungenlied* scholars.

Bäuml, Franz H., and Ward, Donald J. "Zur mündlichen Überlieferung des Nibelungenliedes." *DVjs* 41 (1967):351–90. Together with the following entry, an excellent introduction to the oral-formulaic interpretation of the *Nibelungenlied*.

————, and Spielmann, Edda. "From Illiteracy to Literacy: Prolegomena to a Study of the Nibelungenlied." *Forum for Modern Language Studies* 10 (1974):248–59.

————, and Fallone, Eva-Maria. *A Concordance to the Nibelungenlied, Bartsch-de Boor text*. Leeds: W. S. Maney, 1976.

Bekker, Hugo. *The Nibelungenlied: A Literary Analysis*. Toronto: University of Toronto Press, 1971. The optimistic tenor of the concluding lines of this study may not convince many readers.

Betz, Werner. "Plädoyer für C als Weg zum älteren Nibelungenlied." In *Mediævalia litteraria: Festschrift für Helmut de Boor zum 80. Geburtstag,* edited by Ursula Hennig and Herbert Kolb. Munich: Beck, 1971, pp. 331–41. An important contribution in recent studies advocating MS C as the most "original" *Nibelungenlied* manuscript.

Borghart, Kees Hermann Rudi. *Das Nibelungenlied: Die Spuren mündlichen Ursprungs in schriftlicher Überlieferung*. Amsterdamer Publikationen zur Sprache und Literatur, vol. 31. Amsterdam: Rodopi, 1977. An example of the oral-formulaic approach supported by Cola Minis et al. in Holland.

Brackert, Helmut. *Beiträge zur Handschriftenkritik des Nibelungenliedes*. Quellen und Forschungen, Neue Folge, no. 11. Berlin: de Gruyter, 1963. Takes issue with Braune and others that it is

possible to reconstruct an archetypal *Nibelungenlied* manuscript
which one could then identify with an "original" manuscript.

**Braune, Wilhelm.** "Die Handschriftenverhältnisse des
Nibelungenliedes." *PBB* 25 (1900):1–222. Braune constructs a
stemma for the *Nibelungenlied* manuscript tradition and posits MS
B as the one closest to the "original." Should be read in
conjunction with Brackert's work.

**Bumke, Joachim.** *Mäzene im Mittelalter: Die Gönner und Auftraggeber der
höfischen Literatur in Deutschland 1150–1300.* Munich: Beck, 1979.
A well-written and important work on patrons of the arts in
Germany during the Middle High German period.

**Curschmann, Michael.** *"Nibelungenlied* und *Nibelungenklage:* Über
Mündlichkeit und Schriftlichkeit im Prozeß der Episierung." In
*Deutsche Literatur im Mittelalter: Kontakte und Perspektiven. Hugo
Kuhn zum Gedenken,* edited by Christoph Cormeau. Stuttgart:
Metzler, 1979, pp. 85–119. A sober and highly recommended
study of the oral-formulaic approach to an interpretation of the
*Nibelungenlied.*

**Dürrenmatt, Nelly.** *Das Nibelungenlied im Kreis der höfischen Dichtung.*
Bern: Lang, 1945. Asserts that the *Nibelungenlied* was courtly
poetry and not radically different from the romances of the period.

**Ehrismann, Otfrid.** *Das Nibelungenlied in Deutschland: Studien zur
Rezeption des Nibelungenliedes von der Mitte des 18. Jahrhunderts bis
zum Ersten Weltkrieg.* Münchner Universitäts-Schriften.
Philosophische Fakultät, vol. 14. Munich: Fink, 1975. A good
overview of the reception of the *Nibelungenlied* between 1750 and
World War I. Should be read in conjunction with the studies by
Schulz and Wunderlich.

**Falk, Walter.** *Das Nibelungenlied in seiner Epoche: Revision eines
romantischen Mythos.* Heidelberg: Winter, 1974. Written by a
nonmedievalist, an attempt to understand the *Nibelungenlied* as
"Epochendichtung," as a representative of the time in which it was
written.

**Fechter, Werner.** *Siegfrieds Schuld und das Weltbild des Nibelungenliedes.*
Hamburg: Toth, 1948. One of the more important works to
appear in the immediate postwar period. Controversial, because
heavily influenced by the Scandinavian tradition. Siegfried is
regarded as having defied his own nature.

**Gentry, Francis G.** "Trends in 'Nibelungenlied' Research since 1949: A
Critical View." *Amsterdamer Beiträge zur älteren Germanistik* 7
(1974):125–39. Brief but important overview of major studies
during this twenty-five year period.

Heusler, Andreas. *Lied und Epos in germanischer Sagendichtung.* 1905. Reprint. Darmstadt: Gentner, 1956. Necessary reading for anyone concerned with the *Nibelungenlied.* (See introduction.)

————. *Nibelungensage und Nibelungenlied.* 6th ed. Dortmund: Ruhfus, 1965. A "classic" work in *Nibelungenlied* scholarship in which Heusler, making extensive use of the Nordic analogues, speculates that five authors composed various renditions of the *Brunhildsage* and the *Burgundensage* before a sixth combined both into the *Nibelungenlied* as we have it today.

Hoffmann, Werner. *Das Nibelungenlied: Interpretationen zum Deutschunterricht.* Munich: Oldenbourg, 1969. An excellent introduction to the subject, lucid and concise.

————. *Das Siegfriedbild in der Forschung.* Erträge der Forschung, vol. 127. Darmstadt: Wissenschaftliche Buchgesellschaft, 1979. An especially thorough survey of the various methodologies employed by scholars to "identify" or "classify" Siegfried and the *Nibelungenlied.* All of Hoffmann's work evinces a high level of erudition combined with clarity of presentation.

Höfler, Otto. *Siegfried, Arminius und der Nibelungenhort.* Sitzungsberichte der Österreichischen Akademie der Wissenschaften. Philosophisch-Historische Klasse, vol. 332. Vienna: Verlag der Österreichischen Akademie der Wissenschaften, 1978. Reflects Höfler's belief that myth ultimately lies at the basis of heroic epic. Recommended reading, despite its controversial nature.

Holtzmann, Adolf. *Untersuchungen über das Nibelungenlied.* Stuttgart: Krabbe, 1854. One of the earliest cases made for MS C as the version closest to the "original."

Ihlenburg, Karl Heinz. *Das Nibelungenlied: Problem und Gehalt.* Berlin: Akademie, 1969. A study to be recommended for its perceptive analysis of character motivation as well as for its excellent bibliography.

Körner, Josef. *Das Nibelungenlied.* Aus Natur und Geisteswelt, vol. 591. Leipzig: Teubner, 1921. One of the first studies to examine the *Nibelungenlied* as a work of art molded by conditions prevailing in Germany about 1200.

Kralik, Dietrich. *Die Sigfridtrilogie im Nibelungenlied und in der Thidrekssaga.* Pt. 1. Halle: Niemeyer, 1941. The first of four volumes planned by the author (the latter three never appeared). Kralik maintains that several independent, complete (not episodic) lays formed the basis for each part of the *Nibelungenlied.*

Maurer, Friedrich. *Leid: Studien zur Bedeutungs- und Problemgeschichte, besonders in den grossen Epen der staufischen Zeit.* 4th ed. Bibliotheca Germanica, vol. 1. Bern: Francke, 1969. Contains a stimulating,

if controversial, chapter on *leit* in the *Nibelungenlied* in which
Maurer claims that the person of Kriemhild and the sense of the
*Nibelungenlied* are misunderstood if one does not recognize the
significance of the injury done to the heroine and her honor by
Hagen.

**Mowatt, D. G.,** and **Sacker, Hugh.** *The Nibelungenlied: An Interpretative
Commentary.* Toronto: Toronto University Press, 1967. The
depiction of Hagen's killing of Siegfried as symbolic of a
homosexual act is one of a number of points in this study which
have made it extremely controversial. While not without its
insights, it should be read with caution.

**Nagel, Bert.** *Das Nibelungenlied: Stoff—Form—Ethos.* Frankfurt:
Hirschgraben, 1965. A well-structured discussion of some of the
basic aspects of the *Nibelungenlied* by one of the most
knowledgeable scholars in the field. The section on "Ethos," which
comprises about one-half of the work, is to be particularly
recommended.

**Panzer, Friedrich.** *Das Nibelungenlied: Entstehung und Gestalt.* Stuttgart:
Kohlhammer, 1955. A veritable treasure chest of information.
Reflects the author's belief that heroic epic is ultimately derived
from fairy tale.

————. *Studien zum Nibelungenliede.* Frankfurt: Diesterweg, 1945.
Attempts to illustrate how indebted the *Nibelungenlied* poet was to
French literary works of the period.

**Rupp, Heinz,** ed. *Nibelungenlied und Kudrun.* Wege der Forschung, vol.
54. Darmstadt: Wissenschaftliche Buchgesellschaft, 1976. The
*Nibelungenlied* section contains sixteen essays by leading scholars
offering a broad spectrum of opinions.

**Schröder, Franz Rolf.** *Nibelungenstudien.* Bonn: Kurt Schroeder, 1921.
As Höfler, Schröder contends that heroic poetry is rooted in myth.
See also the following.

————. "Siegfrieds Tod." *GRM* 41 (1960), 111–12.

**Schröder, Werner.** "Die Tragödie Kriemhilts im Nibelungenlied."
*ZfdA* 90 (1960–61), 41–80, 123–60. Schröder demonstrates that
Siegfried is not without guilt for his own fate.

**Schultz, Holger.** *Der Nibelungenstoff auf dem deutschen Theater.* Cologne:
F. Hansen, 1972. A good starting point for anyone interested in
the dramatization of the *Nibelungen* theme.

**Tonnelat, Ernest.** *La Chanson des Nibelungen: Etude sur la Composition et
la Formation du Poème épique.* Paris: Societé D'Edition, Les Belles
Lettres, 1926. Often neglected, but very worthwhile study of the
*Nibelungenlied* with good character analyses.

**Wailes, Stephen.** "The *Nibelungenlied* as Heroic Epic." In *Heroic Epic and Saga: An Introduction to the World's Great Folk Epics,* edited by Felix J. Oinas. Bloomington: Indiana University Press, 1978, pp. 120–143. The influence of Höfler, F. R. Schröder, and Mircea Eliade is clear, but, despite its somewhat esoteric nature for an introductory essay, Wailes's contribution is recommended reading.

**Weber, Gottfried.** *Das Nibelungenlied: Problem und Idee.* Stuttgart: Metzler, 1963. Although Weber's style may cause some consternation, his analyses of leading characters and concepts in the *Nibelungenlied* are insightful and, simultaneously, provocative.

**Wunderlich, Werner,** ed. *Der Schatz des Drachentödters: Materialien zur Wirkungsgeschichte des Nibelungenliedes.* Literaturwissenschaft-Gesellschaftswissenschaft, no. 30. Stuttgart: Klett, 1977. An excellent overview of the *Rezeption* of the *Nibelungenlied* in all spheres from the Middle Ages to 1975.

# Index

Variant forms of proper names are indicated in parentheses after the pertinent page numbers. The introduction has not been indexed.